C000297906

Best wishes

An Irish
Butcher Shop

An Irish
Butcher Shop

Pat Whelan

The Collins Press

First published in 2010 by
The Collins Press
West Link Park
Doughcloyne
Wilton
Cork

Photographs on pp v, vi, viii, ix, x, xx–1, 2, 16, 21, 32–3*, 40, 49, 58, 85,
103, 123, 130, 136, 154, 172, 185, 196, 203, 206, 214, 217, 221, 229,
232, 241 and 244: food stylist Anne Marie Tobin;
photographer: Hugh McElveen.
* With thanks to Malachy Tighe.
All other photographs courtesy Peter O'Donnell

British Library Cataloguing in Publication data
Whelan, Pat.
An Irish butcher shop.
1. Cookery (Meat)
I. Title
641.6'6-dc22
ISBN-13: 9781848890596

Design and typesetting by Anú Design
Typeset in Helvetica Thin
Printed in Italy by L.E.G.O. S.p.A.

Contents

CONVERSION TABLES

Use either metric or imperial measurements in each recipe. Never mix the two.
All spoon measurements are level unless stated otherwise.

Measurements for dry ingredients

1 tablespoon flour	½ oz	15 grams
2 tablespoons flour	1 oz	30 grams
½ cup flour	2 oz	50 grams
¾ cup flour	3 oz	85 grams
1 cup flour	4 oz	110 grams
1½ cups flour	6 oz	175 grams
2 cups flour	8 oz	225 grams
3 cups flour	12 oz	350 grams
4 cups flour	1 lb	500 grams

Measurements for liquid ingredients

¼ cup	1/16 litre	60 millilitres	2 fluid ounces
½ cup	1/8 litre	125 millilitres	4 fluid ounces
1 cup	0.3 litres	300 millilitres	10 fluid ounces
¼ pint	0.15 litres	150 millilitres	5 fluid ounces
½ pint	0.3 litres	300 millilitres	10 fluid ounces
1 pint	0.57 litres	570 millilitres	20 fluid ounces
1¾ pints	1 litre	1000 millilitres	35 fluid ounces

Fan ovens

When using a fan oven, the cooking temperature should be reduced by 20°C.

Preface

Tipperary, immortalised in the wartime song 'It's a Long Way to Tipperary', is perhaps the best-recognised Irish county in the world. Mention Tipperary in Tasmania or Stockholm and it is likely that someone will break into song but know little of the actual area. The place that is Tipperary is one of extraordinary beauty, with ancient mountains, lush, verdant fields and rivers of sparkling water, forming part of the beautiful Golden Vale. Tipperary is blessed with soil that is rich and loamy with a lime content that makes it perfect for nurturing young animals, strengthening bones, and providing premium grazing conditions. County Tipperary is also dotted with horse studs and is home to several of the world's best-known racehorse trainers. Legend has it that the lime content of the soil benefits maturing winners for the sport of kings.

Tipperary has a rich agricultural history stretching back thousands of years. Many towns in Tipperary, such as Cahir and Dundrum, began as forts, built to protect herds of animals from raiding parties. They owe their names to the Gaelic words for fort: *cathair* and *dún*.

These early settled Neolithic farmers had nomadic ancestors who followed herds of wild animals throughout the country and hunted for food as and when they needed it. Food was killed and eaten almost immediately and when it was gone the hunter would have to go out again. It was dangerous and unreliable, often yielding nothing after a day's hunting, therefore highly inefficient. They soon figured out that it would be better to settle in one place and keep the food alive and close by. The animals would get used to humans and could then be killed and eaten as needed. And so the tradition of farming was born. Sheep, goats, horses and a small variety of cattle were left to forage and some were domesticated for consumption, while pigs and hens were part of most households. Such practices were well entrenched by the time the Celts arrived in Ireland around the fifth century BC. Farming was well established, with implements such as the plough already in service.

Even during these ancient, unsophisticated times it was noted that some areas produced better animals and crops than others, Tipperary being one of them. There were no scientific soil tests or environmental studies available then, so people relied entirely on their taste buds. The rest, as they say, is history and, fast-forwarding through the centuries, the tradition of producing excellent food is still thriving in Tipperary county today, although the science behind it has improved greatly. Whether meat, dairy- or crop-based, Tipperary is to natural food what mother is to child; it's a holy union and one that we still benefit from today.

Introduction

It is no surprise to anyone that I have ended up in the business of food. My earliest child-hood memories are of my father taking me to check on the cattle. From the time I could stand, let alone talk, I have been involved in the business of farming animals and selling meat in one form or another. Some say my passion is genetically coded, since I am the fifth generation, maternally, to be involved in farming and meat preparation. It must be in my blood and going into this business for me was as natural as breathing. My father's people were also farmers. When he and my mother met, they found in each other the perfect partner to establish their own business in the meat industry and in 1960 they opened their first butcher's shop.

We lived above the shop, which meant that there was little, if any, separation between work and home. Living above the business was standard practice throughout Ireland when I was growing up and the connection between home and business was absolute. Every time we left the house to go to school or outside to play, we had to go through the shop, inhaling and absorbing the atmosphere, the chat and the *craic*.

Despite the advantages of having family and business so intrinsically linked, it was always my parents' goal to own a farm that could supply the shop. Eventually a property was bought on the outskirts of the town and the vision of owning a farm that provided much of the stock for the shop was fulfilled.

The innovative and creative approach that I'm often credited with is in no small part inherited from my parents and the way they built the business. While other butchers were continuing with the traditional stall, open-fronted with meat hanging from the beams, a fly swat and a few sharp knives at their elbow, my father was investing in chill cabinets and a counter for the shop. His progressive attitude led to him displaying meat in a way that had never been seen before in rural Ireland and he always had one eye on the future. I took it all in from an early age and it was to be the seed for my own personal passion to become the best in the business.

My mother and father were very much a team. How my mother juggled four children, cooking for the butchers who would assemble around our table every day for dinner, as well as maintaining the accounts and 'the book' of orders and dispatch, is a multitasking marvel to this day and one that I now reflect on with awe. As if all this was not enough, she also developed a 'country business', which meant a door-to-door run to the houses and farms located outside the town. Several days a week she would rise early and lay out the boot of her car with various cuts of meat, and then drive off into the countryside, calling on her customers along the way. Her route was the same every week, covering considerable ground around the Tipperary lowlands and mountains. We would get a chance to go with her during school holidays and calling on isolated places, often down bumpy boreens, seemed an adventure every time. Along the way we'd be given a glass of milk here or a piece of cake there. I can still taste the soda bread that one woman used to give to my mother. Wrapped in a tea towel, still warm from the oven, it was an anticipated pleasure that never disappointed. I don't remember who the baker was or even where she lived, but her soda bread lives on in my memory.

In those days there was no way of storing meat for long periods, so it was a service that was really appreciated. Of course it was a service well worth the work involved, since it developed the reputation of the business and when those country customers made the occasional visit to town, they would make their way to the shop.

At such a tender age I soaked it all up without even realising that I was attending the best business, marketing and sales course ever! As we drove along those bumpy roads my mother would explain just how important this part of the business was and I understood that I had a part to play in it. Helping to load up the car, opening and closing entrance gates at farmhouses and listening to the various transactions were all part of my practical education.

Today the business is providing meat to customers beyond the locale in ways that could never have been imagined by my mother. I'm proud to say that James Whelan's Butchers was Ireland's first online meat supplier. We now have an Internet business that has been fine-tuned to the point where we can guarantee that meat ordered before 3.00 p.m. on any given day will be delivered to any address in Ireland the next day. From the top of a mountain in remote Donegal to an apartment in Dublin, meat is presented chilled and packaged ready to cook or freeze. Without leaving the comfort of their homes customers can view the range of meats on offer, receive expert tips, advice and recipes and simply tick a box to ensure delivery. In a way it is the technological equivalent of my mother's original idea, which showed a creativity and ongoing determination to meet the customers' needs, and indeed surpass their expectations with the quality of what we have to offer. I suppose that has been the constant signature trend of our business through the generations and it has stood to us all.

Reflecting on the influence of my parents, I know that their passion for the business and their commitment to best practice was drilled into me constantly. In 1975 I remember going with my father to see the newly completed shopping centre in Galway, one of the first in the country. Clonmel's shopping centre was still in the planning stages and he immediately registered an interest in a shop there. However, he knew that research on the whole concept needed to be completed before he could fully commit. There was so much to consider. For a start, the notion of late-night shopping was beyond imagining in those days. Ireland operated at a gentle pace of life, and the very idea of people shopping for meat after teatime was preposterous.

This journey to Galway was an extraordinary event. Not only was it a school day, but it was a journey on a scale that was beyond the experience of most of my school friends, many of whom would never have been as far as Limerick (a short distance of 50 kilometres). So the idea of travelling to Galway, and on a weekday, was to me and my classmates of Marco Polo proportions.

It was a time when Ireland was confronting enormous change. Supermarkets were impacting on businesses across the country and shoppers were embracing the convenience of extended shopping hours and large car parks. The loss of connection with the food being sold, the absence of product knowledge, the reduced range of meat cuts sold in shrink-wrapped packaging, and the collapse of community connection with local producers and retailers were just some of the trade-offs in the process. Inevitably other small-town traditions were also lost. When I was a child, shops would close one day during the week, as well as Sunday, so that the five-day week was maintained; in Clonmel it was a Thursday. The rhythm of the working day revolved around a main meal in the middle of the day and many businesses closed between 1.00 p.m. and 2.00 p.m. in the afternoon to allow workers to go home to eat. Not only were the supermarkets and shopping centres impacting on the buying habits of Irish consumers, but this 'open all hours' approach was considerably affecting the social fabric of life across rural Ireland. It was certainly upping the pace and there was also a move out of town as shopping centres were starting to appear on the urban fringes, providing a set of unprecedented challenges and opportunities for retailers around the country. After that day of observation and discussion my father proceeded with the establishment of a shop in the new Oakville Shopping Centre in

Clonmel and it is there that the business has developed and transformed into what it is today.

Growing up in the business, one of my first proper jobs was to deliver meat on Saturday mornings on a black bicycle with a big basket on the front. Initially I was thrilled to be such an important cog in the wheels of the enterprise, but the novelty soon wore off when I realised this wasn't an opportunity to get out and about and enjoy the sunshine. Fog, sleet, gales and driving rain were never a reason not to deliver the goods to our special customers. As I pushed my bike through the elements I remember thinking that there had to be an easier way. With the passage of time I look back on it as a worthy apprenticeship, but I've never forgotten that it was pure slog.

Only certain 'important' people were on the delivery run; the local convent, the priest's house and a few others. I remember one of my clients very clearly. After I handed over her meat order she would make a fuss and reward me with stale cake or a broken biscuit, which I would accept graciously and surreptitiously discard. It was an early lesson in something, I suppose; probably that the customer is always right if sometimes insane!

Cattle marts are the modern focus of the local meat industry and have evolved from the weekly fairs that were central to rural life in Ireland for centuries, but have since died out. Everything that was grown and produced was traded and bought at the weekly fair. It was a time when farmers would catch up with the news of the district and enjoy the camaraderie. The cattle marts retain the last remnants of those rapidly disappearing traditions of rural Ireland. Although the marts have reduced in number in recent years, they can still be found in the bigger agricultural towns. One thing is constant, however. Despite the changing times and pace of life there is still great *craic* at the marts, but the business is serious and no place for the faint-hearted. The traders are stockmen who know you by the cattle you bring, what you buy and the style in which you do it. I can only liken it to a stock exchange; sharp wits and a cool demeanour are essential for a successful outcome.

As a child I would often go to the mart with my grandfather and I remember being enthralled by the atmosphere of the place and the antics of the players. One thing was obvious – an off-hand attitude and casual approach were the order of the day. Poker players could learn a thing or two from a clever stockman. The rapid-fire, monotoned mutter of the auctioneer provided a fitting background soundtrack to the real theatrics of the ring. A shrewd buyer would engage his opponent in conversation, the lifting of a finger on to the back of his neck or the subtle tapping of his brow the only sign that he was actually engaged in a bid. The seller would often want to remain anonymous so that the bidders wouldn't know who was selling, so they would sit in the 'sellers' box' to observe and retain their privacy. It was a box with a small hole, perfect for staying under cover. It was very cloak and dagger, the very essence of mystery and intrigue.

Over the last couple of years I've spent time with my father going to the cattle marts. After a lifetime spent in the business he has great wisdom in the buying and selling of livestock and standing beside him at the auctions has been a tremendous commercial education. There is so much more to it than any book could ever reveal. Through him I was properly prepared for the cut and thrust of the auction process. This childhood and adult absorption of the cattle and meat industry serves me every day in my passion to provide the best-quality product in the country. I feel as enthusiastic and excited about the challenges of offering the best possible experience today as I did on my first day in the business. This book is yet another extension of that ideal about providing the best – this time information about meat. Food is one of the most important things in life and by arming people with the proper knowledge I believe they will ultimately make better choices for themselves and their families.

This is the book I would want to read if I knew little about meat and wanted to learn how best to understand it, choose it and prepare it. It has developed from a lifetime of really listening to customer queries, working with animals and preparing food and enjoying every aspect of it, from rearing it, to selling it, to preparing it for the table. In giving you my favourite recipes I feel there is a part of me between the pages of this book and that my choices reveal quite a lot about me. I make no apologies that the recipes are mainly warm, hearty dishes using natural ingredients that are suitable for cooking in large portions to share with family and friends. Isn't that really the best thing about food? My wish is that you will learn that cooking wonderfully tasty meat dishes is not at all the mystery that some would have us believe and the myriad of cuts available makes it a rich and exciting food journey indeed.

God bless and happy shopping, cooking and eating!

what about meat?

What about meat?

Even before the Celts arrived in Ireland, the natives were enjoying a variety of meats ranging from wild game to domesticated goats, cattle, sheep and, of course, pigs. Throughout our history animals have been kept by even the smallest landholder.

Meat is one of those special foods that not only tastes good but is also good for us. Put simply, red meat is the single most intense nutrient-rich food available to human beings. It contains all the essential amino acids required for good health and growth, and, what is more, contains each in exact proportion to the requirements of the human body. Additionally, red meat is a crucial source of iron and trace elements such as zinc and copper, as well as vitamins B6 and B12. It is no coincidence that, as our early ancestors began to include meat in their diet, the human brain grew in size and developed its functions accordingly. The inclusion of meat in the diet really took off after the discovery of fire. Raw meat is practically indigestible and the cooking process is necessary to render meat suitable for humans. However, even before fire, there is evidence that humans had found ways to tenderise meat without cooking it in order to eat it.

The composition of meat is complex. In simple terms it is made up of bundles of fibres that form the 'grain' of the meat. Connective tissue holds the fibres together and merges to form the large silver sheets that join these bundles into muscles. It is the amount of connective tissue in a cut of meat that identifies it. Naturally the areas on an animal's body that do the most work are where the most connective tissue is present: the neck, the shoulders and the legs. Also the amount of work that the muscles do can impact that connective tissue. This is where most of the nutrients are stored, as well as the proteins, elastin and collagen. Collagen dissolves when heated in hot water and becomes gelatine. Long, slow cooking of a cut of meat with an abundance of connective tissue, such as shoulder, shank or brisket, transforms the sinews by loosening the fibres and altering the texture of the meat and converting it into tender mouthfuls. Once we understand how to get maximum taste and tenderness from meat through the cooking process, using methods such as braising, stewing or pot roasting, we can easily make modest cuts into truly memorable eating experiences.

We simply can't have a proper discussion about meat without using the 'F' word: yes, *fat*! It is absolutely fundamental to the taste and tenderness of most meat. Well-reared, pasture-fed animals will have good fat content since they develop a fat covering for warmth when outside in the open air. Generally it is this fat layer that further contributes to the world-renowned quality of Irish beef. The cuts of meat that contain most fat come from the part of the animal that does the least work, such as the loin and the ribs.

Butchers have a high regard for fat because, when heated sufficiently, it melts and moistens the meat, developing the flavours. It is largely the fat tissue in each species that gives beef, lamb, pork and poultry their particular flavours. Without fat, meat is dry and unappetising.

Apart from the indisputable taste issue, there are significant health benefits to fat and this is a fact that is overlooked in today's lean-meat food culture. All natural fats play important roles in the maintenance of good health. In fact, it is most important in fighting infection. Did you know that a bowl of chicken soup, complete with droplets of fat (not skimmed off as is the usual practice today) is known as Jewish penicillin because of its effectiveness in combating infection? It is why mothers the world over serve chicken soup to cold and flu victims. While comfort is no doubt administered by any warm, tasty liquid, the curative elements are found in the chicken fat.

We have been so indoctrinated into the evils of fat that the very word itself is pejorative and rarely used in a positive sense. I believe that most people confuse fat with trans fats, the evils that result from industrial processing. Trans fats should be avoided at all costs but there are true health benefits in fat that occurs naturally. The fat of nature can be enjoyed without conscience, in my opinion.

Most butchers and chefs agree that for maximum flavour and tenderness meat should be cooked with fat, which should be removed after cooking as required. The type of fat most highly regarded by cooks is the marbling characteristic present in beef and, to a far lesser extent, in pork and lamb. Marbling results from fat between the bundles of fibres making up the muscles and is a dependable indicator of the quality of the meat. The cooking process draws out the marbled fat, melting it and causing it to naturally baste the meat, which adds to the overall flavour and succulence of the cut.

The colour of meat an animal produces is decided by the way the animal has been reared. The presence of muscle fibre dictates whether it is red or white and the movements of the animal decide the level of muscle fibre present. Chickens and turkeys tend to move suddenly but briefly, so use their muscle fibres accordingly. Lactic acid is an essential part of this process and white cells are therefore present that give colour to the muscle. On the other hand, animals that graze and are constantly moving require muscle fibre appropriate for endurance. Red muscle fibres are necessary for stamina, so are present in animals that are constantly moving, such as cattle and sheep or fowl that fly, such as migratory birds and ducks.

From farm to butcher

Let there be absolutely no doubt whatsoever that keeping animals in a stress-free environment contributes significantly to the quality of the meat they produce. The most stressful experience the animal will ever face is the manner in which it is slaughtered. It has always been my mission that the welfare of the animal and the integrity of the whole process of meat production adhere to best practice at all times. Yes, the welfare of the animals is important to me because I have respect for them, but the bottom line is that their care ultimately impacts the quality of meat that I sell and my reputation is determined by that standard of excellence. By sticking to a very strict code of best practice I know that I can provide the best-quality meat that it is possible to offer. There is a tremendous peace of mind when you know that you can stand over every cut.

When cattle arrive at an abattoir, every effort should be made to be as humane as possible. An 'open-barn' pre-slaughter policy, where the animals are left to fast for twenty-four hours, always achieves the best results. The cattle have the freedom to walk around on a dry straw bed with access to copious amounts of water. They can eat as much straw as they like, since the fasting period is not about starvation but rather elimination in order to minimise any contamination from faeces in the slaughtering process.

The animals are brought to be slaughtered in a singular fashion that is a feature of an artisan approach. At all times the animal's welfare is the most important consideration. The area should be calm and the process should be relatively quiet, with no shouting or yelling. In industrial-scale abattoirs animals are lined up and processed in a production line. It is a noisy, clamorous atmosphere and there is no doubt that the cattle are spooked by what is happening around them. This stress will translate immediately into a tense animal, with locked muscles and consequently tougher meat.

The cattle we slaughter are kept hundreds of yards from the slaughter pen and are taken down individually. If for any reason an animal is nervous, we won't go through with it. The animal is removed from the process and returned to the shed until it is at ease. This is what you could call a win–win; the animal is stress-free and it produces better meat as a result.

Today people talk about food miles, meaning the distance travelled by food products

from production to point of sale. I am thrilled to say that in my business we can measure our process in food metres – our abattoir is on site. The animals are not herded into a truck and driven miles for slaughtering, as is standard practice in industrial-scale production.

Thankfully I am not the only butcher in the world who is taking such care. There are plenty of us around, but you have to seek us out. Consumers should never be afraid to ask butchers about their meat supply and the way the animals are reared and slaughtered.

Butcher to fork

Dry-ageing meat is fundamental to its flavour and texture and this applies particularly to beef. Traditionally in Ireland beef has always been aged by hanging it in a controlled, closely monitored cool room for two to three weeks. This is the method of choice for artisan butchers, who recognise that the methods of the past are still the best methods today. When a carcass is hung, the natural enzymes present in the meat work on the muscle fibres, making them softer. After a period of hanging the muscles relax, resulting in more flavoursome meat. The process also allows flavour to naturally develop intensively, leading to the defining characteristic of great meat – *taste*!

However, hanging carcasses in a cold room for twenty-one days where it inevitably loses body weight does not make economic sense to many industrialised processors. Industrial processors use water in the primary process to clean the carcass and I believe this leads to spongy, poor-quality meat for the consumer. Additionally, excess water will leach out of the meat during cooking, resulting in poor eating quality.

In our modern world we have sadly come to a place where most large-scale retailers who serve the masses care more about marketing than meat. The usual commercial focus is on shelf life and packaging convenience. The language of traditional butchers is used and exploited for the benefit of the consumer, but the method is different. Often a premium cut of beef is labelled 'aged' when in reality it is vacuum packed and sitting in a plastic bag of blood. A good butcher has complete knowledge of the entire process from field to shop window. He will hang the beef until he is certain that it has reached maximum readiness.

How meat is cut also impacts directly on the quality of the finished product and great skill and experience are required to achieve a premium result. The artisan butcher takes time to achieve the best possible product that matches consumer expectations. In contrast, supermarkets and the industrial approach to meat mean that speed and thrift are the primary concerns and machinery is often used to prepare meat.

When an animal is butchered, it is first cut into large sections called 'primal cuts'. These are broken down into smaller sections known as 'sub-primals' and then into retail cuts such as roasts, steaks, chops and so on. A butcher who hangs his own meat in a cool room can offer the cook the full range of cuts. A good butcher will also suggest cooking methods that maximise the taste. One of the great losses to a generation of supermarket shoppers is the knowledge of just what to do with anything other than steak or mince. The range offered by supermarkets is limited because of mass production at the processing plants and the lack of knowledge of the staff selling the meat. Indeed in many places you are choosing directly from a self-service chill cabinet without a qualified butcher in sight. Talking of supermarket chill cabinets, another 'advancement' in the food production arena is the introduction of Modified Air Packaging (also known as Modified Atmosphere Packaging or MAP) to prolong shelf life. I particularly dislike this technique, because I believe that most consumers are unaware of the process. In this so-called preservation technique the air that naturally surrounds the food in the package is changed to another composition. By taking away the natural air the deterioration of the product is slowed down. However, while it is a common practice, we should be aware that, to change the composition of the air inside the pack, a type of gas is pumped in (depending on the product, the packaging and the storage temperature). This method is commonly used in large-scale production to prolong the shelf life of meat, fish, cheese, fruit and vegetables. In the case of meat it is easy to spot a MAP product, since it is usually marketed in a tray with a firmly sealed film lid. This is a common practice and, while it has been passed as safe, in my opinion it is not 'natural'. The less tampering done to my food the better, so buying a product that has been sitting around in a tray of gas renders it more processed than I like it to be.

There is a strong connection between lean meat and slightly tougher cuts in relation to flavour: if cooked correctly, tougher meat is likely to be more flavoursome. If cooked on the bone, there is an additional dimension and intensity of flavour to the meat due to the release of marrow from the bone into the juices.

It is a fact that full-flavoured meat comes from fully grown animals. As the animal ages, more connective tissue develops due to the amount of exercise and movement accumulated. A younger animal will provide more tender meat, since there is a direct correlation between the amount of connective tissue present and the degree of toughness.

In past times older animals were consumed only when they had long passed their usefulness for providing milk, wool or eggs. Long, slow cooking was found to transform these tough old beasts into tender, delicious meat. Slow cooking is a method common to all cultures, with variations in the flavourings through spices and vegetables the distinguishing element. I'm delighted to report that slow cooking is seeing a renaissance and there is a whole 'Slow Food movement' gaining ground throughout the world. The Internet has provided a fantastic platform and method of communication for devotees and there are excellent articles and resources about the subject freely available online.

People lead busy lives, and this demands that meat be lean and tender for quick cooking convenience. The choice of meat has been reduced to the cuts that can be grilled or fried in minutes. These cuts are now viewed as superior to traditional choices such as beef shin or lamb shanks. However, many of you may be very surprised to learn that there is no ladder of taste in meat as long as the various cuts are cooked appropriately. Trust me when I say that the humblest meat cut can become a feast if cooked long and slow. There is much pleasure in this method, as the anticipation of the meal ahead grows and usually the aromas of the bubbling pot or pan fill the kitchen. The luscious juices are enriched by the dissolved gelatinous texture of the meat, and the sticky, richly coloured sauce is an added dimension to the meal.

Slow cooking is being appreciated by a growing number of home cooks who are realising that it is not the cooking preparation that is long, but simply the time it takes once in the oven. Just twenty minutes or so is all that is required to get the meat and vegetables into the pot, and then the dish takes care of itself, with rewards of flavour far greater in proportion to the time taken to prepare it.

I know I sound as if I'm on a soap box for traditional butchers but nothing, I'm afraid, can replace the care, knowledge and experience that are brought to the chopping block at your local butcher's and the premium cuts that result.

Storing meat

The optimum storage of meat is something that many people are not aware of. It is a constant frustration for butchers or indeed any fresh food retailer. Meat and fresh produce regularly leave a shop in perfect condition only to be left for too long in a hot car on the journey home, resulting in a product that reaches the fridge in less than ideal condition. It should be put in the fridge at home as soon as possible and the temperature maintained at a constant rate.

In most homes the storage place for meat, the fridge, is also the place where many of the items used continuously throughout the day are stored, so it is accessed repeatedly. With every opening of the fridge door the temperature is raised, which has a cumulative negative impact on the shelf life of any foodstuff stored, including meat.

There are two ways to store meat to keep it in the best possible condition: by freezing it immediately on getting it home directly from the point of purchase, or by keeping a fridge specifically for protein. This may seem unrealistic for a domestic kitchen, but it need only be a small bar fridge kept solely for that purpose. They are readily available these days at reasonable prices.

Probes are now standard equipment for the measurement of fridge temperature and are also easily obtained. I would recommend that every home should have such a measuring device in the fridge to ensure that safe levels of refrigeration are constantly maintained. To my mind, freezing meat is an excellent option when considering storage. It is a product that freezes well and the advantages are obvious. You have a ready store for unexpected occasions and you can bulk-buy for convenience and, quite often, value. The key to the successful freezing of meat is to get it into the freezer as quickly as possible after purchase and to keep air from getting to the meat while it is in the freezer.

I want to temper the above with the following: it is a myth that, once meat is frozen, it keeps indefinitely. My customers often ask me about this, feeling that there is no need to consider just when the meat was placed in the freezer. For best results meat should be dated on the day it is frozen, as oxidation and dehydration of meat continue even at freezing temperatures, albeit very slowly. Most home freezers are set higher than the optimum −18°C/0°F, so deterioration will definitely occur over time. The optimum time to use frozen meat is within a month of purchase, although periods of up to a year would be acceptable for beef and lamb; it's about six months for pork.

Thawing meat is a process that should be carefully considered, as bacteria are ever present in every environment and should be avoided if possible. The meat to be thawed should be placed on a large dish to avoid any possibility of drips on to other food. It should be thawed out overnight in the fridge and it is vital to ensure that it has thawed completely before cooking. A large joint will take longer than twenty-four hours to thaw, and two days should be allowed to ensure that it is ready for cooking. Of course, busy lifestyles dictate that meat is often defrosted in the microwave, which is perfectly safe, although the end result is definitely taste-compromised.

If using meat fresh from the fridge, there are some differences to consider between the various types of meat purchased. Minced meat is best cooked on the day of purchase, as are poultry and offal. Beef, lamb and pork can be stored for days before cooking, with one of my customers who has a regular order of a fillet of beef holding it for eleven days at home before cooking because he enjoys the fully developed flavours, and it is his preferred taste.

One of my pet hates is the bewildering variations in the language used regarding the safe shelf life of food. Visit a supermarket and you find such advice as 'best before', 'use by', 'packed on', 'display until' and so on. As I have often speculated, does it mean that at one minute to midnight on the 'use by' date a product is safe to consume, and at one minute past midnight it is not? Obviously the advice is there for the consumer's protection, but I recommend a degree of common sense when judging whether food is ready for consumption by the use of Mother Nature's free gift and essential guide, the nose!

ways
to cook
meat

Our Irish ancestors from the Bronze Age developed an ingenious method of cooking large joints of meat in boiling water by building stone-lined trenches near a water source to fill them from. Large stones heated in a nearby fire would be thrown into the water which would heat up accordingly, and joints of meat would then be dropped into the liquid until cooked to taste. These cooking sites or *fulachta fiadh* can be found all over Ireland.

Each cut of meat requires a certain method of cooking and choosing the correct technique is always the key to a satisfying outcome. The leanest steak will be dry and tough if cooked for too long, while cuts that are densely packed with connective tissue will become melt-in-the mouth delicious when cooked for hours at the right temperature. Below I have outlined the various methods used throughout the book and farther on I have included recipes that use cuts of meat that are less fashionable, but when cooked long and slow are feasts to savour. Often these cuts are very economical.

Roasting

The Sunday roast has been part of our tradition for generations, still holding an appeal for even the most jaded of diners. Premium quality meat cooked in this way is always a winner because of the delicious natural flavour of the meat that is drawn out during the roasting process. It is a very reliable way to cook meat with cooking times adjustable according to taste.

True roasting used to be meat cooked on a revolving spit in front of an open fire with a pan placed underneath to catch the drippings. Today's roast is cooked in the oven, so it is probably more accurate to say it is baked rather than roasted, but basting the joint with the drippings throughout cooking means that there is much that is similar to the original method and explains why the term 'roasting' has been retained.

When roasting meat in the oven it is important to choose a pan that is sturdy enough to withstand time on top of the stove for the gravy-making stage. It is also important to bring refrigerated meat to room temperature about thirty minutes before placing it in the oven. In order to calculate the cooking time accurately you have to know the weight of the joint, so weigh the meat and work out how long it is going to take. Set the oven to high with the shelf towards the bottom. Always preheat the oven for at least fifteen minutes. Put three tablespoons of oil into the pan and then add the meat. When the oven has reached the desired temperature, place the pan into the oven and leave it for thirty minutes or so. This sears or seals the surface, producing a crusty finish. With beef I like to give it that initial thirty minutes at 245°C/475°F/gas mark 9, then fifteen minutes per 500 g/1 lb after that, adding another fifteen minutes for medium rare and thirty minutes for well done. Don't forget that the joint will also need time to rest once it is out of the oven. You will find a table of meat, times and temperatures at the end of this section.

Stuffing the joint or bird to be roasted is a matter of choice, and needs to be considered in the timing of the roasting process. Stuffed meats are usually cooked to well done and benefit from having some piquancy to give them interest.

Basting the roast throughout the cooking time is to be recommended. Basting a chicken provides a crispy browned skin and the crackling of pork also benefits from basting by becoming crisper and golden. To baste the meat, take the pan out of the oven and place it on a board. Spoon the hot dripping over the meat several times and return to the oven. Consider, though, that every time the oven is opened and the meat removed for basting, cool air gets in and the cooking is slowed. For fatty joints such as legs of lamb it is not necessary to baste at all.

The key to a successful roast is the resting period after the meat is cooked. Remove it from the roasting pan and place it on a warmed plate and allow it to stand for at least twenty minutes before carving. The resting period allows all the internal juices to redistribute throughout the meat. Many of them will have risen to the top during the cooking process. The same applies to roasting red or white meat. By leaving it to rest for the appropriate time it will carve easily and the joint will be moist throughout. Don't worry about it going cold; it will retain its heat during the resting period.

I would always recommend that the gravy should be made from the juices left in the pan after the joint has been removed. If fat was added to the roast for cooking, tip some of it off and put the pan over a low heat on the stove top. Scrape up the bits of meat that are stuck to the pan and press into the juices that remain, adding salt and pepper to taste. If adding flour for thicker gravy, add a tablespoon of flour to the scrapings and remaining juices and add a little water or red wine if there is some to hand. Bring the liquid to a gentle simmer and cook for a few minutes to ensure that the flour is incorporated. Add any juices that have leaked from the resting meat. Just how thick you like your gravy is a personal choice and there are no hard or fast rules. However, if you are making the gravy in the roasting pan as suggested, add the flour in small amounts. It is much easier to thicken up gradually than to start thinning out.

So just how do you know when the beef is done? The definitive way to detect whether a roast has reached the right temperature is to use a thermometer. Meat thermometers are inexpensive to buy and you will find them in any good kitchen shop or online. They really are an invaluable aid for any cook. Insert the thermometer into the thickest part of the joint, away from the bone. Leave the thermometer for thirty seconds to get an accurate reading.

Beef can range from 45°C (113°F) if you want it very rare to 75°C (167°F) for well done. Pork, which needs to be cooked through, should always read 75° C (167°F). Lamb can be treated as beef. The following table can be regarded as a relatively reliable time frame.

TOTAL COOKING TIMES

Oven temperature	Times
Beef 180°C/350°F/gas mark 4	**Rare:** 15 minutes per 500 g/1 lb plus 15 minutes more **Well done:** 20 minutes per 500 g/1 lb plus 30 minutes more
Lamb 180°C/350°F/gas mark 4	20 minutes per 500 g/1 lb plus 20 minutes more
Pork 180°C/350°F/gas mark 4	30 minutes per 500 g/1 lb plus 30 minutes more

Note: Ovens are a little like cars – while you can drive any car, you will always be most comfortable driving your own. Each car has its own particular feel and so does an oven. The above table is only a guide. Get to know your oven and adjust accordingly.

Pot roasting

This is one of the simplest and best methods for cooking a cheaper cut of meat. The long, slow cooking renders tougher cuts tender, moist and tasty. However, it is vital to have the right equipment and ideally a Dutch oven or enamelled cast iron pot with a firmly fitting lid that is big enough to hold a joint comfortably will do the job perfectly.

Pot roasting is all about first browning the meat and then adding vegetables of choice and cooking slowly. If there is insufficient fat on the joint, add about two tablespoons of oil to the pot and brown the meat on all sides. For an easy meal, just add an onion stuck with two cloves, a bouquet garni and salt and pepper. There is no need to add any liquid unless stated in the recipe, and then only a cup or so. Cover with the lid and place over a very low heat or in a slow oven, allowing about thirty minutes per 500 g/1 lb. Pot-roast meat is served like roast meat, ideally carved into slices and drenched with gravy full of the flavours from the joint.

Braising

Braising is a cooking method that can transform a tougher (and therefore cheaper) cut of meat into a memorable meal. Because these cuts have more connective tissue, the long, slow cooking breaks down the tendons and muscle fibre into a gelatinous, delicious food, creating tender melt-in-the-mouth meat drenched in a delicious sauce. These enhanced flavours and wonderful textures are achieved because the meat is cooked out completely and, when combined with the vegetables, herbs and spices that are added to the pot, the result is extremely satisfying.

Braising is a combination of steaming and baking, as the food is cooked, ideally, in a heavy cast iron pot with a firmly fitting lid. The meat is browned and sealed right at the beginning of the cooking so that it caramelises on the surface and enhances the flavour. To achieve this, the pan should be heated before adding the oil or butter and then the meat. Once browned, the meat is put aside and any root vegetables being used placed into the pot. These should be gently sautéd in the remaining oil for fifteen minutes with the lid on the pot. The meat is then placed on top of the vegetables with any liquid being used, and cooked in the oven at 160°C/320°F/gas mark 3 for two to three hours or on top of the stove on a low heat for the same amount of time. The meat is served with the gravy strained and poured over it.

Frying

Frying is a popular method of cooking because it is quick and suits busy lifestyles. There are two methods of frying: deep-fat and shallow-fat frying. Most meats are shallow-fried

rather than deep-fried, and it is often the first stage of braising and pot roasting.

There is a range of fat and oil options that match the type of cooking and the natural flavours of the meat. A combination of butter and oil is ideal for most meats with clarified butter (ghee) used for curries or olive oil for a Mediterranean flavour.

Frying is often done in a saucepan or flameproof casserole as well as a frying pan. It is essential for a good result that the cooking utensil being used has a heavy base which will distribute the heat evenly and fry the meat without burning or sticking.

If shallow-frying meat in a frying pan, the oil should cover the base of the pan. In the case of crumbed cutlets the oil should come up the side of the pan so that the sides of the meat are completely cooked.

First fry the side of the meat to be seen on the plate and then turn the meat once only during cooking. If the meat is thick, it should first be browned on a high heat and then cooked through on a moderate heat. Any brown sediment left in the pan after the meat is removed should be used if possible. Excess fat can be poured off and the pan reheated with a little water or wine and then poured as gravy over the meat. It is a pity to waste any of the tasty and nutritious juices.

Tip: You may not always have an open bottle of red wine to hand for gravy and sauces, so keep an ice-cube tray filled with an inexpensive red table wine in the freezer. Four to five average-size wine cubes give half a glass of wine, but it will obviously depend on the type of ice tray you use. Once taken out of the freezer they melt pretty quickly and will do so even faster once they hit a hot pan. These cubes are also handy to drop into casseroles and stews.

Grilling

Grilling is a quick and simple method of cooking good-quality, tender cuts of meat, which results in tender, juicy, full-flavoured dishes. For the diet-conscious it is the perfect method of cooking, since the meat is cooked without the addition of any fats or rich thickened sauces.

Ideally meat should be grilled over a charcoal grill (and no, this is not barbecuing). It is common, however, to grill under a gas or electric grill. In this case heat the grill first until it is red hot. Leave the grill rack in the oven while heating, since raw meat will not stick if put on to a very hot griddle. You can also buy some wonderful standalone health grills these days. I think they can be a little gimmicky, as you will achieve the same result with the grill in your oven, but for ease of use they are pretty good.

Brush the meat with a little oil and pepper if required. It is recommended not to add salt because this causes the juices to run out, losing some of the flavour and moisture in the meat. Place the prepared meat under the red-hot grill and cook until it changes colour from red-pink to brown, which should take about two minutes. Turn the meat over using tongs rather than a fork, as the prongs can pierce the meat and cause a loss of juices. Sear the other side and continue cooking until the degree of doneness is achieved.

Times for grilling meat depend on the cut, the type of meat, the thickness and, most of all, personal taste. Grilled meat should be served immediately. It is not necessary to let it rest.

GRILLING TIMES

Cuts	Minutes
Rump steak (Sirloin) 680 g/1½ lb slice, 2.5 cm/1 inch thick Serves 3–4	Rare: 6–7 Medium rare: 8–10 Well done 14–16
Sirloin steak (Striploin) 2.5 cm/1 inch thick Serves 1	Rare: 5 Medium rare: 6–7 Well done: 9–10
Minute steak (thin slice of entrecôte) 1.25 cm/½ inch thick Serves 1	Rare: 1–1½ Medium rare 2–3 Well done: 5
T-bone steak 4–5 cm/1½–2 inches thick Serves 2–3	Rare: 7–8 Medium rare: 8–10 Well done: 11–12
Porterhouse steak 4 cm/1½ inches thick Serves 1–2	Rare: 7–8 Medium rare: 8–10 Well done: 11–12

Fillet steak 2.5–4 cm/1–1½ inches thick Serves 1	Rare: 6 Medium rare to well done 7–8
Pork chops	15–20
Lamb chops	8–10
Sausages	Thin: 8–10 Thick: 10–15
Bacon rashers	3–4

Barbecuing

There is something about the aromas of a barbecue that stirs the gastric juices. Cooking meat over a flame or charcoal is as fundamental as it gets and was the method employed by our ancestors. However, despite its seeming simplicity, many a meal has been ruined by cooking on a heat that is too high or over flames that scorch the delicate flesh of the meat. I think we have all experienced the barbecue from hell where the chicken is charred black on the outside but displays a frightening underdone pink on the inside, making it inedible. Patience is required to achieve the unsurpassed taste of well-barbecued meat, as the heat is perfect when all the flames have died down and only embers remain. Here again you will find your meat thermometer invaluable.

Most meats can be cooked successfully on a barbecue, although some require careful attention to avoid reducing them to blackened chunks of unidentifiable matter. Meats that do well with barbecuing are chops, steaks, burgers and sausages. If closely monitored, satays and kebabs are also suitable. Marinating meat for the barbecue is a simple way to ensure that the meat is well lubricated and impregnated with wonderful flavours.

Like ovens, barbecues vary, whether it is a traditional charcoal grill or a modern gas affair. Either way, get to know your own barbecue. Don't wait until all your party guests are assembled to light it for the first time.

Stewing

Stewing is a favoured method of cooking for dishes that are as easy to prepare as they are delicious. The wonderful juices that are part of the meal are especially enjoyed soaked up with chunky bread or mashed potato.

The meat should be cut into pieces and cooked in a minimum of liquid. A stew can be cooked on the stove top or in the oven, with the temperature kept low enough to keep the liquid just simmering, as a rapid boil will toughen the meat.

Meat stews can be either brown or white. In a brown stew the meat is browned in oil or fat and flour is sometimes added and browned to give extra colour and flavour. Stock is added to come just below the level of the meat, and the pan or casserole is always covered.

In a white stew (also called a fricassée) the meat is not browned, but often blanched first to whiten and remove any strong flavours, as in a traditional Irish stew. A white stew is cooked on top of the stove and is thickened after the meat is cooked.

Stews that have been cooked long and slow have a rich intensity of flavour because of the extraction of juices from the meat and vegetables and the breaking down of the connective tissue in the meat.

If the liquid has not evaporated sufficiently, the temperature can be increased or the casserole uncovered to reduce it. Add only a small amount of salt to begin with, since any reduced liquid will retain all the salt. Adjust seasonings at the end of the cooking process if necessary.

Because a stew is simply a combination of solid food ingredients that have been cooked in liquid and served in their own gravy, it is an internationally recognised method of cooking and every country has its own version. Hungary has goulash, Lancashire hotpot is served in England, *pot au feu* is a French stew, Mexico has the *barbacoa*, in Morocco it's a *tagine*; the list is as long as there are countries. A stew will be tastier if made the day before serving and gently reheated.

Stir-frying

Stir-frying has become very popular in the Western world. Meat or poultry is cut into thin strips and fried quickly in a wok or heavy pan at a very high heat. It is really important to heat the pan before adding the oil and, once the oil is added, to make sure that the whole pan is coated. Ideally the oil should be smoking when you add the meat.

If using beef, only cuts such as tenderloin will do and it should be cut into thin strips.

The meat should be sizzled briefly, browning the outside, and cooked through completely if using pork or chicken. Marinating the meat adds to the flavour, but the meat must be relatively dry when it hits the pan.

Stir-frying has been perfected by the Asian community but the Western world is embracing this cooking technique as a fast and healthy way to cook food. Spices such as garlic, ginger and chillies often appear in stir-fries.

Equipment

You don't need me to tell you about the value of good knives or cookware – it is a subject that has been discussed to death by chefs and cooks the world over. However, there are kitchen items that I feel are worth highlighting. I have been amazed to find that some really keen cooks will have a fancy *flambé* torch hidden somewhere at the back of a cupboard and yet will never have considered buying a meat thermometer. How many kitchens boast those little hand-held whisks for frothing coffee or an expensive electric tin-opener that is rarely used and yet don't own a simple pair of tongs? So here is my list of simple basics that seem to have escaped many. Apart from one or two items, most things are inexpensive and easily found.

Meat thermometer

Take the guesswork out of cooking and buy a meat thermometer. It will prevent you over-cooking food and, more importantly, undercooking it, which can pose a serious health risk. A meat thermometer can be used for all foods and not just meat. It measures the internal temperature of cooked meat, poultry or casseroles to ensure that a safe temperature has been reached. By cooking food to the proper temperature you eliminate the possibility of harmful bacteria that cause food poisoning. Once you get used to using one, you will use it all the time. There are several types available on the market. Make sure that the thermometer you buy is designed for meat and poultry. I recommend a stainless steel thermometer with a clear shatterproof lens and easy-to-read dial, but digital thermometers are also available. For poultry, insert the meat thermometer into the inner thigh area near the breast of the bird, but avoid touching the bone. For beef, pork and lamb the thermometer should be inserted into the centre of the thickest part of the meat, again away from the bone. I use my meat thermometer all the time and find it particularly helpful when barbecuing.

Kitchen timer

These little gems are worth their weight in gold. Mine is a small, light, digital affair. It certainly works hand in hand with the meat thermometer for getting things right. While I don't rely on it completely, it is a super guide. It is particularly invaluable when you need to baste a joint regularly throughout the cooking process, letting the timer alert you at every basting interval. They don't cost a great deal and I would recommend something simple and digital for precision.

Kitchen tongs

How many times have you stabbed a steak with a sharp knife or fork in order to turn it over in a pan? First of all, this action pierces the meat and releases the juices that you are trying to seal in for flavour. With a thinner piece of meat, such as a slice of bacon, stabbing it with a knife or fork risks damaging the base of the pan you are using. Or how about trying to remove something from boiling water, balancing it precariously with spoons and forks, only for it to drop right back into the pot? A simple pair of kitchen tongs will solve these problems instantly. I have to admit that the pair I use are some kind of heat-resistant plastic and came free with a bag of rice. There are several different types available on the market: wooden, plastic or stainless steel. Don't underestimate the usefulness of kitchen tongs. They are very inexpensive compared to their worth in a kitchen and the inconvenience and pain of burnt fingers.

Kitchen scissors

Every house has a pair of scissors except when you need them! In the kitchen scissors are fantastic. While every chef will tell you the value of great knives, and I agree, they often neglect to mention the humble kitchen scissors. Kitchen scissors, also known as kitchen shears, are similar to common scissors, but there is a difference in that kitchen scissors have the fulcrum located farther from the handles to provide more leverage and thus more cutting power. High-quality kitchen scissors can easily cut through the breastbone of a chicken and other forms of meat with hard, dense bones. They come to the rescue in battles with packaging. You can snip and trim certain meat cuts and vegetables more easily with scissors than you can with a knife. The uses are endless. However, I would stress that kitchen scissors should be kitchen scissors. Please avoid other uses, such as trimming the dog's hair, the kids' art projects or the myriad of other household uses that a family finds for scissors. Kitchen scissors should be just that. While you don't need a gold-plated pair, I would explore the scissors market and go for a good sturdy pair. They might cost more than your average discount centre household job, but they should last for a long time.

Dutch oven

You will see mention of a Dutch oven at times throughout this book. I believe this is one of the essential items for a family kitchen. It is really just a large casserole pot, but, rather than a glass casserole dish, a Dutch oven is a thick-walled iron (usually cast iron) cooking pot with a tight-fitting lid that can be used on top of the oven as well as in it. My only advice is to invest as much as you can afford in this item. As a brand name Le Creuset has possibly the best reputation for such items, but they are certainly a considered purchase. However, they will outlive you if you look after them and might even be considered treasured family heirlooms of the future. You can find good-quality, less expensive alternatives, but I would be wary of a very cheap model. This item is worth saving for.

Garlic press

A garlic press is designed to crush garlic cloves efficiently by forcing them through a grid of small holes. Garlic presses present a convenient alternative to chopping garlic with a knife. In the world of chefs garlic crushed by a press is generally believed to have a different flavour from garlic minced or chopped with a knife. The press-crushed garlic is believed to release a stronger flavour. Some chefs prefer them; they believe you get a finer finish and better all-round distribution throughout a dish. Other chefs believe them to be at best useless and at worst an abomination. I love mine, which is good-quality stainless steel. You should find one easily anywhere kitchenware is stocked.

Tip: If you get garlic or onion residue on your fingers, just dip them into a bowl of salt, rub gently for a second or two and rinse. The smell will disappear immediately.

Roasting tins

Having a selection of roasting tins is necessary, since you need to use a tin appropriate to the size of the piece of meat you are cooking. I would say at least a large and a medium size should be in every kitchen. Again go for quality over quantity, but make sure that it can be used on top of the hob as well as in the oven – always very handy for the gravy-making stage. For this reason good-quality metal-based tins are the most versatile and shouldn't buckle under the heat of a hot plate. Sadly, you do get what you pay for when it comes to these items, so go for the best you can afford.

Roasting rack

I like to use a rack when I am cooking meat so that the air can circulate around the joint while the juices are preserved in the pan. Using a wire rack with handles is also very useful when taking the meat out of the roasting tin.

Quality oven gloves

Meat juices are hot. Roasting dishes are hot. Skin burns and your hands are irreplaceable. Yet despite these obvious facts some people prefer to risk it with a rolled-up tea towel! I'm not going to say any more on the subject other than 'Get proper oven gloves'. They are cheaper than skin grafts and avoid hours spent in A&E!

And finally…

After the above I can only recommend that you invest in the best-quality pots, frying pans and knives you can afford. When it comes to knives I prefer to buy them individually rather than in a set. What many people find is that in a domestic setting they use two to three knives for everything and the rest are unused. With most cookware you really do get what you pay for, but there is a very good middle market available today. Many famous chefs have endorsed excellent lines, but be aware that occasionally you are paying extra for the celebrity name tag. My personal recommendation is to do some research, particularly when you are investing in the bigger-ticket items such as pots, pans and knives. If I'm ever in the market for something new I tend to research it first online, consult with my cooking friends and then go to a shop to see and hold it physically. How something feels in your hand is very important, since some things may look very good but will be impractical for everyday use. Preparing food to nourish yourself or an entire family is one of the greatest gifts and wonders in life. Don't dishonour such a noble undertaking by using poor equipment.

beef

Farming in early Gaelic Ireland was dominated by cattle, and Irish myths and epic tales reveal the reverence with which they were regarded, which went far beyond cattle being merely an important food source. Cows were the measure used to assess the value of land and social status, and to pay fines. During the ninth century a tribute paid to the Kingdom of Cashel consisted of thousands of cows, as well as pigs and sheep.

In early medieval Ireland a person's social status was marked in cattle units as outlined according to Brehon law, which was established in the sixth century. It was common to describe a woman 'of 4 heifers' or a man of '3 milch Cows' and so on as a way of establishing hierarchy.

When the size of one's cattle herd was an indication of social status, maintenance of the herd was central to the way of life. Cattle-raiding was a standard occurrence and a newly crowned king was expected to demonstrate his leadership qualities by executing a royal raid immediately after taking the throne.

Ireland's earliest beef cattle were small, hardy animals that roamed freely, grazing unhampered by any system of husbandry. Brought to Ireland by one of the many waves of settlers from Europe thousands of years ago, these original Irish cattle thrived in the cattle-perfect conditions on the island.

Over the past few centuries, Continental breeds have been brought to Ireland and late-maturing, very lean beef has been produced from a range of cattle such as Limousin, Simmental, Charolais and Blonde d'Aquitaine. However, the national preference for tender marbled meat has led the Irish beef industry to concentrate on Irish Hereford and Irish Angus, bred over time from English Hereford and Aberdeen Angus stock. These are the cattle we farm and sell from our shop in Clonmel.

The Angus is a Scottish breed, originating from northeast Scotland. Because of its origins it is a hardy animal, very compact and naturally palled (it never grows horns). It winters well in harsh conditions and thrives in the lowlands and lush grasses of Tipperary.

The primal cuts of Angus beef are smaller, so portion cuts are consequently small. As a steak it is excellent enjoyed medium or rare, when the flavour can be really appreciated. When rolled, the roast beef isn't an enormous piece; it is a tighter roll that makes for an excellent roast.

The Hereford is a distinct breed of animal again. Originally from England, it has been bred in Ireland since the early 1800s and produces the highest-quality red marbled meat from grass. It has similar qualities to Angus, although it is not naturally palled. The marbling that occurs in the Hereford is the characteristic that really adds quality to the product and makes for tasty, tender beef. All chefs look out for the marbling in red meat and know that, when cooked, the marbled fat melts and moistens the meat, with the resulting depth of flavour transporting the meat in quality to its highest level.

Producers breeding and farming our cattle cross the Angus breed with Hereford bulls, which results in a smaller animal. The calf grows to maturity in eighteen months, the optimum stage for slaughter. Because the Angus and Hereford are so hardy, they thrive outside and can feed on grass and hay throughout their lives. The temperate Irish climate means that the cattle bred here have a natural healthy diet of grass, giving them the best conditions in which to thrive.

Grass versus grain

There is a distinct difference between the nutritional benefits of grass-fed and grain-fed cattle. Meat from grass-fed animals has up to four times more omega-3 fatty acids than meat from grain-fed animals. Omega-3 fatty acids are a vital component in the maintenance of good health and, of all the fats, omega-3s are the most heart-friendly.

Meat and dairy products from grass-fed animals are also the richest known source of another type of important fat cell, 'conjugated linoleic acid' or CLA, which is an exceptional omega-6 fat shown to be beneficial to healthy body maintenance. Many food producers now proudly boast the CLA content of certain products as a selling point and a way to distinguish their products in a crowded marketplace. Additionally, meat from grass-fed animals is found to be up to four times higher in vitamin E than those that are grain-fed.

Many scientific studies have been carried out to support these claims, but even without such backup it makes sense that raising livestock on open pasture, where animals are free to roam and eat a variety of natural grasses and plants, is better than being caged, confined and fed a boring diet of nothing but grain.

Our grass-fed animals are treated holistically from birth to the finished product ready for sale. They are raised with integrity, and consideration for the welfare of the animal is always the guide. Today quality is paramount in Ireland and Irish grass-fed cattle reared without artificial hormones according to EU standards are a highly prized commodity in foreign markets.

While studies provide proof of health benefits from grass-fed animals, I would also contend that you will find a noticeable difference in taste and texture as well. Searching out good grass-fed beef will enhance your taste experience and ensure that the animal's welfare was always top of the agenda. A definite win–win for all concerned.

Finding quality beef

When looking for good-quality beef, colour is one of the first indicators. The meat should be dark red in colour (closer to claret than bright red) and springy to the touch, with a light, sweet scent. Good beef should have a covering of fat and veins of creamy fat threaded through the grain, called 'marbling'. Melted fat is the primary taste enhancer in any joint and, if it has a good layer of fat, you won't need to pay so much attention to basting it during the cooking process, saving time and effort. When we talk about the marbling we mean delicate and thin veins in abundance rather than a few thick streaks, which can indicate that the animal has been poorly fed.

The domination of supermarkets over small specialty shops in the retailing of food has changed much that is obvious to even the casual observer. One of the biggest impacts of supermarkets on the consumer is the loss of contact with a person who is expert at what they do, be it growing and selling vegetables, making and selling cheeses, or butchering and preparing cuts of meat.

Along with the loss of expertise is the disconnection between the customer and the origin of the food. Sad to say, there is also plenty of documentation of children living city lives who have to be told that potatoes don't just come in plastic bags, or that milk comes from a cow and not a carton. But nowhere is this more obvious than in the meat sector.

Over the past few decades butchers' shops have disappeared in their hundreds from the retailing landscape and with them the immediate connection for the consumer with what they are buying and cooking. In times past, when a visit to the butcher's shop was often a daily experience, or at least a weekly one, the customer would enter a place where animal carcasses swinging from a hook at the back of the shop were part of the experience, and the connection with the animal clearly understood. The butcher, with his vast knowledge of the cuts of meat and how to cook them, was the friendly and informal educator of the consumer.

With the arrival of supermarket self-service shopping and shrink-wrapped meat on plastic trays, already diced or minced, the average supermarket customer immediately lost their source of information and service and with it came a gradual loss of knowledge. A generation later, there are very few consumers who have any knowledge at all about the origin of various meats, let alone the different cooking methods and suitable cuts. Ignorance of cuts beyond mince and steak has meant that some people are now daunted by the thought of entering a traditional butcher's for fear of displaying their dearth of knowledge and in the process they are losing the opportunity to try different cuts of meat as well as free advice on the best ways of cooking it.

On the other hand, there is growing interest among consumers in the provenance of what they are purchasing because of a search for better nutrition and taste. Recently supermarkets have introduced language such as 'artisan-produced', 'grown locally' and 'hand reared' into their marketing and advertising to give customers the notion of quality. Increasing awareness of the importance of food integrity and quality has seen supermarkets incorporate some new product lines that meet the criteria of artisan production to appeal to this new awareness. However, the meat you find in a butcher's shop almost always differs from the supermarket due to the fact that it has been hung. Beef must be hung for three to four weeks to mature and in the process the carcass naturally loses a substantial amount of its initial weight. This cost is carried by the butcher and therefore the price of beef is sometimes marginally greater at a butcher's than in a supermarket. The gain is at the table, since meat properly hung will not shrink as much when cooked. We have all had the bad experience of roasting a large joint of meat only to discover that it has shrunk beyond recognition when finished and there is a lot less meat than originally anticipated. Don't get caught out, buy what you can afford. A cheaper cut from a good butcher that requires slower cooking and more attention will always taste better than a more expensive joint from a cheaper source.

Which cuts?

There is no ladder of 'nicer' or 'better' meat. If cooked appropriately, any cut of good beef will be delicious. Price is often based on supply and demand. Sometimes the more expensive cuts are just the ones that will cook quickly and therefore are more in demand.

Beef cuts are described as being from the hindquarter or the forequarter. In general terms, the hindquarter provides the best cuts for quick cooking, with the forequarter cuts benefiting from slow, wet cooking. Specifically, the amount of connective tissue in the chosen cut dictates the cooking method that best draws out the qualities of that cut. Tender cuts with little connective tissue are best roasted, fried or grilled and tougher cuts with more connective tissue (and in turn more flavour) reach gourmet status when cooked slowly, as in braising, stewing or pot roasting.

Beef recipes

The thing I remember most about my childhood is that it was one of warmth, good food and lots of people around the table. Dinner was always provided for the butchers who worked in the shop below, so there were meals served constantly between noon and 3.00 p.m. Steaming food in vast quantities, loud chat and plenty of *craic* and laughter meant that our home was always one where people gathered and shared food. As a small boy I always enjoyed sitting with the men and feeling a part of the grown-up world. It was a bit like a restaurant in that the table was never set for fewer than twelve and there seemed to be a constant flow of diners. My siblings and I always saw ourselves as part of the team and we all had specific jobs that seemed entirely reasonable at the time. One of mine was setting the table and for a small child it seemed a never-ending task – no sooner would the table be cleared from dinner than it would need to be set again for tea.

Every morning at school I eagerly anticipated the piping-hot cooked dinner that would be waiting for me. In those days we ate our main meal in the middle of the day, a time that most of us now consider lunchtime. I would run home with stomach rumbling and I was never disappointed. It was steaming hot, hearty, wholesome food and I knew even then that I was fortunate. From visiting friends' homes I was aware that it wasn't like this for everyone. It is hard to beat the combination of having a father who was a great butcher and a mother who was an excellent cook.

Good food experiences create powerful memories. Many of those memories from my childhood remain favourite meals today.

Steak and Kidney Pie

Nothing can compare with my mother's steak and kidney pie. I still use the same recipe with just a small tweak; where she would have used lard or dripping to cook the meat, I use olive oil. As an all-round favourite, steak and kidney pie ticks all the boxes. It's a very satisfying dish that also freezes well for a delicious midweek treat without any fuss.

Serves 6

2 sheep's kidneys, washed, skinned, halved, core removed, cut into 1.25 cm/ ½ inch cubes

500 g/1 lb stewing steak (blade, flank, skirt or round), cut into 2.5 cm/ 1 inch cubes

3 tablespoons plain flour

1 teaspoon salt

freshly ground black pepper

2 tablespoons olive oil

½ cup water

2 tablespoons parsley, finely chopped

1 quantity flaky pastry (see page 246)

1 egg, beaten

Preheat the oven to 220°C/425°F/gas mark 7.

Put the flour and seasonings into a plastic bag and add the steak and kidney pieces, shaking to cover well.

Heat the oil in a heavy pan and brown the meat, stirring constantly for about 5 minutes. Add the water, cover tightly and simmer for at least one hour or until well cooked. Cool and stir in the parsley.

Roll out the pastry until it is slightly larger than the lid of the pie dish. Cut a strip about 2.5 cm/1 inch wide and place it around the dampened rim of the dish. Brush with cold water and spoon the steak and kidney mixture into the dish, then cover with the remaining pastry, pressing into the pastry rim to seal.

With thumb or knife end press a pattern around the edge of the pie and glaze with the egg, making a hole in the middle to allow the steam to escape. Bake in a hot oven for 20 minutes (220°C/425°F/gas mark 7), then lower the heat to moderate (180°C/350°F/gas mark 4) and cook for a further 30 minutes or until the pastry is golden.

Of course the pie should be served with lashings of mashed potato or sometimes champ, where scallions are finely chopped and cooked in a little milk and then mixed through the creamy spuds. (See recipe for champ on page 212.)

Roast Rump with Garlic and Red Wine Gravy

Garlic is an ingredient that finds its way into many of my recipes. It is not that long ago that the notion of including a chopped clove of garlic in a dish would have seemed alien to most of us. This may seem like a lot of garlic, but it really does add an extra dimension of taste and the red wine added to the gravy lifts it to a very special roast.

Serves 6

2 kg/4½ lb rump roast
3 cloves of garlic, peeled
    and cut into 6 long slivers
1 tablespoon olive oil
salt and pepper
1 medium onion, peeled and
    cut into quarters

Gravy
¼ cup red wine
2 tablespoons plain flour

Preheat the oven to 190°C/375°F/gas mark 5.

If there is time, remove the joint from the fridge at least 1 hour before cooking. When the meat is ready, make 6 small incisions on the top and place a sliver of garlic in each. Pour the oil on to the meat and massage it in with your hands. Season with salt and pepper. Place the onion in the pan and position the meat on top, fatty side up, so that the fat melts and self-bastes the joint, creating the juices for the gravy. Place in the oven.

After 30 minutes or so reduce the temperature to 180°C/350°F/gas mark 4 and continue cooking for 1½ hours or longer, depending on taste. Test by removing from the oven and checking the colour of the juices. For well done, the juices should be clear. When done to your liking, remove the meat from the oven and leave it to rest on a warmed plate for 15 minutes. It is worth remembering that meat will continue to cook while it is resting.

While the meat is resting, pour any excess fat from the pan and place the pan on top of the stove over a medium heat. Add a little water and the wine to deglaze the pan, incorporating all the browned bits from the cooked meat that may have lodged around the edges of the pan. Add the flour, a little at a time, stirring quickly to avoid lumps. When the flour looks like a paste, add additional water, depending on the thickness of the gravy required, and adjust the seasoning to taste.

This is an easy joint to carve and can be sliced and placed on a platter with the gravy poured sparingly over the slices to present at the table.

Beef Bourguignon

I can clearly remember the first time I enjoyed this classic dish. I was pleasantly surprised that it was so much more layered in taste than my expectation, which was that it was just a beef stew with a fancy name. I was wrong. The aromas that fill the house when it's cooking stimulate the appetite every time.

Serves 6

3 tablespoons olive oil

175 g/6 oz streaky bacon, chopped

1.5 kg/3 lb stewing steak, cut into 2.5 cm/1 inch cubes

2 medium onions, peeled and finely sliced

1 medium carrot, peeled and sliced

1 bottle red wine

2 cups of beef stock or 2 stock cubes in 2 cups water

2 tablespoons tomato paste

bouquet garni made from a bay leaf, a sprig of thyme, 2 parsley sprigs, 4 cloves of garlic and 2 cloves bundled together in cheesecloth and tied securely

salt and pepper

The casserole can be cooked on the stove top or in the oven. If you are cooking it in the oven, preheat it to 180°C/350°F/gas mark 4.

Heat the oil in a pan and fry the bacon until well browned. Remove to a heavy-based casserole. Add the beef to the very hot oil in the pan and brown all over quickly until well sealed and, using a slotted spoon, add to the bacon. Add a little more oil to the pan if necessary and add the onions and carrot. Cook until the onions are aromatic and add this mix to the casserole. Deglaze the pan with the wine and pour into the casserole with enough beef stock to cover the meat. Add the tomato paste, the bouquet garni and the salt and pepper and cover tightly. Simmer over a low heat on the stove top or bake in the oven for 2–3 hours until the meat is well cooked.

With 30 minutes or so left to cook, add a little oil to a frying pan and brown the shallots all over, then remove from the pan. Add the mushrooms to cook for a few minutes.

Remove the casserole from the heat. Place a sieve or colander over a saucepan and strain the casserole

18 shallots, peeled and
    kept whole
500 g/1 lb small button
    mushrooms, cleaned
3 tablespoons plain flour
35 g/1¼ oz butter at room
    temperature
parsley, finely chopped, to
    garnish

mixture, discarding the vegetables and bouquet garni.
Return the meat to the saucepan with the strained liquid
and add the shallots and mushrooms. To thicken the
sauce, mix the flour and butter to a paste and, with the
pan off the heat, gradually whisk through.

Gently reheat, adjust the seasoning and serve with
parsley sprinkled over the top.

Braised Beef and Guinness Casserole

Guinness – or stout by any other name – adds a lushness to this dish and the prunes offset any bitterness of the stout with just a hint of sweetness. The oil and butter combination helps to brown the meat and develop crusty caramelised bits that really enhance the flavour when incorporated into the sauce. I love this served with buttery mashed potatoes to soak up the juice.

Serves 6

1 kg/2 lb 4 oz braising beef, cut into 2.5 cm/1 inch cubes

4 tablespoons plain flour seasoned with salt and pepper

2 tablespoons olive oil

4 streaky bacon rashers, chopped

2 large onions, peeled and chopped

15 g/½ oz butter

2 cups Guinness (or any stout, but not lager!)

2 bay leaves, a sprig of thyme and a sprig of parsley tied together into a bouquet garni

8 prunes

½ cup parsley, finely chopped

Preheat the oven to 180°C/350°F/gas mark 4.

The easiest way to coat the meat in the flour is to toss it in a plastic bag and shake until the cubes of meat are well coated.

Heat the oil in a sturdy pan and gently brown the bacon. Remove from the pan and place in a casserole dish. Add the onions and fry until they are aromatic and beginning to brown, moving them around to avoid burning. Add these to the bacon in the casserole. Melt the butter in the pan, add the beef and cook until browned all over. Then add to the bacon and onions in the casserole. Keep the pan over the heat and pour in half the Guinness, scraping up any residue, and bring to the boil. Pour this over the meat and add the bouquet garni. Add the rest of the Guinness to the casserole with enough water to ensure that the meat is just covered. Cover the casserole with a tight-fitting lid and place in a moderate oven (180°C/350°F/gas mark 4) for 2 hours.

After 2 hours take the casserole out of the oven and stir. Add the prunes and cook for a further 30 minutes. Check for seasoning and remove the bouquet garni before serving. Stir in the parsley and serve.

Braised Oxtail

There has been an upswing in demand for oxtail as people rediscover its pleasures. It has to be cooked long and slow, resulting in a thickened rich sauce and melt-in-the-mouth texture. The dish takes around 4 hours to cook, but the preparation takes only a fraction of that. The wonderful aromas that waft through the house as this dish looks after itself prepare everyone for the feast ahead.

Serves 6

50 g/2 oz plain flour seasoned
    with salt and pepper
4 oxtails, cut into pieces
2 tablespoons olive oil or
    30 g/1 oz butter
    (or combination of both)
2 medium onions, peeled
    and thinly sliced
2 thick bacon rashers,
    chopped
2 garlic cloves, peeled and
    finely chopped
570 ml/20 fl oz red wine
1 litre/35 fl oz beef stock
bouquet garni of a bay leaf,
    a sprig of thyme, a sprig
    of parsley and a sprig of
    rosemary, tied together
2 medium carrots, peeled
    and diced
2 celery stalks, sliced
2 tablespoons tomato paste
    salt and freshly ground
    black pepper
½ cup parsley, finely chopped

The casserole can be cooked on the stove top or in the oven. If you are cooking it in the oven, preheat it to 180°C/350°F/gas mark 4.

Put the seasoned flour into a plastic bag and add the oxtail pieces. Shake it well to coat the meat. Heat the oil or butter in a large heavy-based casserole and add the oxtail pieces in small batches. As each batch is browned, remove to a warmed plate with a slotted spoon and repeat until all the meat has been sealed. Add a little more oil if necessary and add the onions and cook until golden. Add the bacon and garlic and cook for 2–3 minutes. Return the meat to the casserole, pour in the wine and simmer until the liquid has reduced by about a third. Add the stock and bouquet garni to the pot and cover. Simmer gently on the stove or cook in the oven for about 2 hours.

At this point add the carrots, celery and tomato paste and continue to cook for a further 2 hours or so, until the meat falls off the bone. Adjust the seasoning and sprinkle with chopped parsley and serve with mashed potatoes and baked parsnips.

Crumbed Steak with Mustard Sauce and Avocado

Crumbed meat is always popular and at the shop we have ready-to-go options for busy people. For those who want to get their hands dirty, the result is well worth the effort and the process is quite therapeutic.

Serves 4

4 fillet steaks

3 tablespoons plain flour seasoned with salt and pepper

2 eggs, beaten

3 cups fresh white bread-crumbs

3 tablespoons fresh parsley, finely chopped

50 g/2 oz butter

2 tablespoons olive oil

2 avocados, peeled and sliced

Mustard Sauce

3 egg yolks

1 tablespoon lemon juice

salt and pepper

2 teaspoons Dijon mustard

125 g/4½ oz butter, softened

To make the mustard sauce, place the egg yolks, lemon juice, seasonings and mustard into a double saucepan (a bowl over a saucepan of hot water will work equally well if you don't have a double saucepan) and stir until combined. Add the softened butter and mix well. Place the saucepan over a low heat and stir until the sauce is thick and creamy.

The steaks need to be thin in order to cook through quickly, so first remove any fat from each steak and pound out to about 1.25 cm/½ inch thick.

Have three wide bowls or dishes ready and a plate to receive the finished crumbed steak. One bowl contains the flour, the second is for the beaten egg mixture, and the breadcrumbs and chopped parsley go into the third. Taking each steak separately, coat with the flour first and then dip it into the egg mix. Finally, press the breadcrumb/parsley mixture on to the steak and place it on a plate. Repeat until all steaks are covered. Refrigerate the crumbed meat for at least an hour until ready to cook. Heat the butter and oil in a large pan and cook the steaks until golden brown, about 3 minutes on each side.

Plate up with slices of avocado on top and a trail of the mustard sauce.

Slow-cooked Beef Pot Roast

At weekends when we just want to relax with the kids and enjoy a meal together with not too much time taken to prepare it, this is often our first choice. It takes only 15 minutes or so preparation time and then it's left to cook slowly for hours with only the effort of plating up involved.

Serves 6

2 tablespoons olive oil

1.5 kg/ 3 lb of beef
    shoulder/blade roast

1 large onion, peeled and
    sliced

4 cloves of garlic, peeled
    but left whole

3 medium carrots, peeled
    and cut into large chunks

2 celery stalks, sliced

3 potatoes, peeled and
    cut in half

½ cup red wine

salt and pepper

parsley, finely chopped,
    to garnish

In a heavy-duty cast iron pan such as a Dutch oven heat the oil on a medium heat and when it is very hot add the meat and leave for a few minutes on each side, turning to brown and seal it. When the meat has browned all over, remove it to a plate. Add the vegetables and sauté until the onion is soft. Add the wine and seasoning and return the beef to the pot. When it reaches simmering point, reduce the heat and cover the pot with a tight-fitting lid. Let it cook for 3 hours or so until the meat is very tender, then lift the meat on to a warm serving platter, cover and keep warm.

Turn the heat high to reduce the liquid to a thick sauce. Strain the sauce and serve poured over the beef. Garnish with parsley and serve with boiled potatoes.

A bunch of flavouring herbs may also be added, such as marjoram, thyme, parsley and bay leaf tied with string. Lift out and discard after cooking.

Osso Bucco

Shin of beef is one of those cuts seldom used in recent times by the average cook. The deeply flavoursome meat is bound by much connective tissue and when cooked long and slow melts and causes the sauce to become a taste event in itself, and that's before sampling the meat! If you were a fan of the classic TV show The Sopranos, *this Italian dish was one of Tony Soprano's favourite meals.*

Serves 6

8 slices beef shin, cut at
    least 2.5 cm/1 inch thick
plain flour seasoned with
    salt and pepper
85 g/3 oz butter
2 tablespoons olive oil
1 medium onion, peeled
    and finely chopped
3 celery stalks, chopped
2 medium carrots, peeled
    and chopped
4 garlic cloves, peeled and
    finely chopped
1¼ cups white wine
1 x 220 g/8 oz can of
    chopped tomatoes
1¼ cups chicken stock
3 tablespoons parsley,
    finely chopped
finely grated zest of 1 lemon

Coat the beef shins well with the flour. In a heavy-based pan melt the butter and add the oil. When the oil and butter are very hot, fry the beef until browned all over. Remove the beef to a warmed plate and add the onion, celery, carrots and half the garlic. Cook until soft and aromatic. Return the beef to the pan and add the wine. Cook uncovered for 15 minutes or so. Add the tomatoes and stock, then cover with a close-fitting lid and simmer for 1½–2 hours.

Mix together the parsley, lemon zest and remaining garlic and stir in before serving.

Persian Koftah
(Beef and Rice Meatballs)

A friend of mine who is passionate about Middle Eastern cooking introduced me to this simple dish and it has all the elements of comfort food that I love. The rice and split peas in this meatball and tomato dish will stretch a small amount of mince into a meal that could feed ten people. However, it needs to be planned ahead, since the split peas and rice have to be soaked for several hours before using.

Serves 6

1 cup split peas, soaked in
    water for 5–6 hours
1 cup basmati or long-grain
    rice, soaked with the peas
500 g/1 lb minced beef
1 large onion, peeled and
    finely chopped
4 eggs, beaten
2 tablespoons fresh tarragon,
    finely chopped
1 tablespoon mint, finely
    chopped
1 tablespoon parsley, finely
    chopped
salt and pepper
sunflower oil for frying
2 x 220 g/8 oz cans
    chopped tomatoes
2 tablespoons tomato paste

Preheat the oven to 180°C/350°F/gas mark 4.

Drain the peas and rice. In a large bowl combine them with the meat, onion, half the beaten egg, herbs and seasoning. Mix well and form into balls. Use the remaining egg mixture to coat each meatball. Heat the oil in a large pan and add the balls in batches and cook until golden, but not necessarily cooked through.

Combine the tomatoes and the tomato paste. Place the koftah (meatballs) into a casserole dish and cover with the tomato mixture. Cook in the oven for 1½ hours or so, until the tomato sauce has been absorbed. It may be necessary to add a little more liquid during cooking.

Beef Wellington

This is one of those retro dishes that conjure up notions of sophisticated dining using the best silver and crystal. It is time-consuming to prepare rather than difficult. I love to cook it from time to time, as I always receive appreciative responses from impressed diners for what is actually a very straightforward dish, especially if you take the shortcuts of using bought pâté and ready-made pastry!

Serves 6

1 whole beef fillet
2 tablespoons olive oil
35 g/1¼ oz butter
225 g/8 oz field mushrooms,
    chopped into small dice
salt and pepper
500 g/1 lb pâté
6 slices of Serrano ham
500 g/1 lb puff pastry
1 egg, beaten with
    1 teaspoon water

Red wine sauce
150 ml/5 fl oz red wine
60 ml/2 fl oz beef or
    chicken stock
30–50 g/1–2 oz cold
    butter, cubed

Preheat the oven to 220°C/425°F/gas mark 7.

The meat should be left out of the fridge for 30 minutes or so to bring it to room temperature. Rub the oil into the meat and place it into a roasting pan and then into the oven for 20–25 minutes for medium to well done. The timing is about taste preference, so adjust it accordingly. When the meat is cooked, remove it from the oven and let it cool completely, reserving the pan juices along with any sediment.

Heat the butter in a separate pan, add the mushrooms and stir until all the liquid is evaporated and the mixture is dry. Season to taste and leave it to cool.

Spread the fillet with the pâté, covering it completely. Lay out a large piece of clingfilm and on top of that line up the slices of ham. Place the pâté-covered fillet on top and spread the mushroom mix over it. Wrap the ham around the fillet and then roll up tightly in the cling-film and refrigerate for about 30 minutes.

Roll out the puff pastry into a rectangle larger than the fillet. Unwrap the fillet from the clingfilm and place it on

the pastry. Brush the edges of the pastry with the egg mixture. Fold up the long edges of the dough to enclose the sides, pressing together to seal. Fold the ends that have been brushed with the egg mix and press together.

Transfer the fillet to an oven tray and place it seam side down. Chill in the fridge for an hour so, and then place in the oven and cook for 30 minutes or until pastry is puffed and golden.

To make the red wine sauce, pour the wine and stock into the reserved juices in the roasting tin on top of the stove and deglaze over a medium heat, incorporating all the crusty bits. Boil to reduce the stock by about a third, add the cold butter and stir until the sauce has heated through.

Meat Loaf

Everyone should have a meat loaf recipe in their repertoire. Served hot with vegetables it makes a great dinner, but cold and sliced it is perfect picnic or buffet food. As it is cooked without any added fat or oil, it's also a healthy option for the diet conscious.

Serves 6

500 g/1 lb best beef mince
250 g/9 oz pork sausage
　　meat
1 cup fresh breadcrumbs
1 large onion, peeled and
　　finely chopped
1 egg, beaten
3 cloves of garlic, peeled
　　and finely chopped
3 tablespoons parsley,
　　finely chopped
2 tablespoons sun-dried
　　tomato paste
salt and pepper
olive oil or butter to grease tin

Preheat the oven to 180°C/350°F/gas mark 4.

Using half the breadcrumbs, put all the ingredients into a bowl and mix until well combined. Lightly grease a loaf tin and then press the meat mix into it. Now press in the remaining breadcrumbs. Cover the tin with aluminium foil.

Alternatively, form the mixture into a loaf shape, roll in the breadcrumbs and wrap in aluminium foil. Place in a baking dish and roast for 1½ hours. If cooking in the tin, remove the foil 30 minutes before the cooking time is up to brown the top.

Beef Olives

For a good economical but filling dish, beef olives ticks all the boxes.

Serves 4–6

6 thin slices topside steak
2 tablespoons olive oil
1 medium onion, peeled
    and finely chopped
1 tablespoon plain flour
1½ cups beef stock or water
1 teaspoon salt
freshly ground black pepper
pinch grated nutmeg

Bacon and herb stuffing

2 bacon rashers, finely
    chopped
1 small onion, peeled and
    finely chopped or grated
15 g/½ oz butter
1½ cups soft breadcrumbs
2 tablespoons parsley, finely
    chopped
½ teaspoon each of dried
    thyme, marjoram and sage
½ teaspoon salt
freshly ground pepper
1 egg, beaten
cornflour to thicken (optional)

First make the stuffing. Heat a frying pan, add the bacon and cook until almost crisp. Add the onion and butter and continue to fry until the onion is soft. Put the breadcrumbs, herbs and seasoning into a bowl and add the bacon mixture. Add sufficient egg to bind the stuffing.

Trim the fat off the meat and cut the slices into the required number of pieces. Place the beef between two pieces of plastic or baking paper and beat until thin. I find a rolling pin is ideal for the job. Spread the stuffing on each slice of beef, roll it up and tie with string. Heat the oil in a heavy saucepan or casserole and brown the beef rolls quickly on all sides, then remove the beef olives and keep them warm.

Lower the heat, add the onions and cook until soft. Then add the flour and cook for 1 minute or so. Add the stock or water, salt, pepper and nutmeg and bring to simmering point. Return the beef olives to the pan and reduce the heat to low. Cover with a tightly fitting lid and simmer for 1½–2 hours or until the meat is tender. To serve, lift the meat on to a serving dish and remove the string. Thicken the gravy if necessary with a little blended cornflour or reduce over a high heat. Pour over the beef olives and serve.

Satay Beef

I love barbecuing and these skewered satays are very popular with children. When barbecuing meat, brush it with oil before placing it on the hotplate, rather than pouring the oil on to the barbecue where it can cause flames and burning. Also soak the wooden skewers in water while the meat is marinating to prevent them burning when cooking.

Serves 6

1½ tablespoons soy sauce

2 teaspoons cornflour

2 tablespoons brown sugar

1 teaspoon fresh ginger, peeled and grated

1 tablespoon water

700 g/1½ lb rump steak, cut into 4 cm/1½ inch cubes

4 tablespoons olive oil

satay skewers

Satay Sauce

30 g/1 oz butter

1 medium onion, peeled and finely chopped

2 cloves of garlic, peeled and crushed

1½ teaspoons mild curry powder

¾ cup roasted unsalted peanuts, blended or processed finely

2 tablespoons soy sauce

1 red chilli, seeds discarded and finely chopped

1½ cups water

Combine the soy sauce, cornflour, sugar, ginger and water in a bowl. Add the meat and mix well. Let the meat marinate for at least 1 hour. Thread the meat on to the skewers and brush it with the oil. Barbecue until browned all over.

To make the sauce, melt the butter in a pan, add the onion and garlic and cook for a few minutes until aromas develop. Add the curry powder and the peanuts. Stir for 1 minute and then add the soy sauce, chilli and water. Bring to the boil, reduce the heat and simmer uncovered for 10 minutes until thick.

Satay sauce also makes a great topping for jacket potatoes.

Chilli Con Carne

This is a simple, hearty dish that is a good alternative to spaghetti bolognese. The chilli content can be modified according to taste. The red kidney beans are a great addition, offsetting the power of the chilli while giving a textural lift to the dish.

Serves 6

1 tablespoon olive oil

1 large onion, peeled and finely chopped

3 cloves of garlic, peeled and finely chopped

1 red pepper, deseeded and finely chopped

2 teaspoons ground cumin

1 teaspoon paprika

1 heaped teaspoon hot chilli powder

500 g/1 lb minced beef

400 g/14 oz chopped tomatoes, fresh or canned

3 tablespoons tomato paste

salt and pepper

400 g/14 oz can red kidney beans

Heat the oil in a saucepan over a medium heat, add the onion and cook until translucent. Add the garlic, pepper and spices and stir. Simmer for a few minutes until well combined and the aromas of the spices are evident. Add the mince to the mixture and break it up as it is stirred into the vegetables and spices. Cook until the meat is well browned. Add the tomatoes, tomato paste and seasoning and simmer for 30 minutes or so, checking the liquid and adding a little water if it reduces too quickly.

Add the kidney beans and stir in. Continue to cook for another 10 minutes or so until the beans are well incorporated.

It's great served with plain rice. Put the rice in a bowl and spoon the chilli over the rice. Top with a spoonful of sour cream to finish off.

Beef Stew with Dumplings

I always consider this winter food. Of course it is delicious at any time of the year but somehow it's perfect on a cold, dark, wet evening. Dumplings always add a comforting dimension and are perfect for soaking up the gravy.

Serves 6

4 tablespoons plain flour
  seasoned with salt and
  pepper

1 kg/2 lb 4 oz braising steak,
  cut into 2.5 cm/1 inch
  cubes

4 tablespoons olive oil

2 large onions, peeled and
  finely chopped

2 medium carrots, peeled
  and sliced

2 celery stalks, sliced

1 turnip, peeled and cut
  into cubes

570 ml/20 fl oz beef stock

2 bay leaves

2 tablespoons fresh thyme
  leaves or 1 teaspoon
  dried thyme

Dumplings

175 g/6 oz plain flour

2 teaspoons baking powder

½ teaspoon salt

2 tablespoons oil

½ cup milk

Put the seasoned flour in a plastic bag, add the beef cubes and toss to coat.

Heat the oil over a moderate heat in a large saucepan or flameproof casserole dish and add the beef cubes. Brown well on all sides. This should be done in batches, removing the meat from the pan to a warmed plate until all the meat is browned. Add the onions and cook until they start to turn translucent and add the rest of the vegetables, stirring frequently to brown. Now return the beef to the pan and add the stock, bay leaves and thyme. Bring to the boil, stirring well. Cover tightly and reduce heat to as low as possible. Simmer for at least 2 hours.

To make the dumplings, sift the dry ingredients into a bowl and add the oil and milk. Stir until the dry ingredients are incorporated and the mixture resembles a batter. Mould the dumplings into small balls. Approximately 15–20 minutes before serving, turn up the heat, bring to the boil and drop the dumplings on to the surface of the stew. If the stew is being cooked in the oven, allow around 30 minutes for the dumplings to cook.

Beer-basted Barbecue Steaks

Most barbecues in our household are spontaneous events, but marinating meat for the barbecue gives a degree of certainty about the taste and tenderness of the end result, particularly if you are uncertain about the tenderness or indeed the taste of the meat at hand.

Serves 6

¼ cup brown sugar
1½ tablespoons grainy mustard
1 tablespoon white wine vinegar
1 cup beer (ale or lager can be used)
1 medium onion, peeled and finely chopped
1 bay leaf
6 steaks, trimmed

Place the sugar, mustard, vinegar, beer, onion and bay leaf in a saucepan and bring to the boil. Reduce the heat and simmer gently for 10 minutes, uncovered. Cool. Pour the mixture over the steaks. Stand for 2 hours or so, turning occasionally. Barbecue until cooked as desired.

Corned Beef and Cabbage

I love corned beef. Eaten warm the first day and then in a sandwich on the second day spread with my favourite mustard makes for a grand treat.

Serves 6

1.5 kg/3 lb salted silverside
   or topside of beef
1 medium onion, peeled
   and stuck with 4 cloves
bouquet garni of a bay leaf,
   a sprig of thyme and a
   sprig of parsley
2 medium onions, peeled
   and quartered
1 medium carrot, peeled
   and chopped
1 cabbage, trimmed and
   cut into quarters

Soak the meat in cold water overnight. Drain off the liquid and put the meat into a large saucepan and cover with water. Add the clove-studded onion and the bouquet garni and bring to the boil. Reduce the heat to a simmer and cook for 1½ hours.

Add the onions and carrot. After a further 15 minutes add the cabbage and cook for another 15 minutes or so. Drain the pot and remove the onion and the bouquet garni.

Serve the meat sliced, accompanied by vegetables and boiled potatoes.

Stir-fried Beef and Greens

The preparation of ingredients for stir-frying often takes longer than the cooking itself. This is because all the ingredients must be cut to a uniform size so that the cooking can be accomplished quickly and evenly. A wok is excellent for stir-frying because its high sides let you stir and toss the ingredients briskly. Use long cooking chopsticks or a wooden spatula to keep the ingredients moving around. Oh, and make sure to chop and prepare all the ingredients before attempting to cook them. Many a good stir-fry has been ruined through too much frying and not enough stirring because the chef is still chopping.

Serves 6

3 tablespoons soy sauce

2 tablespoons dry sherry

1 tablespoon brown sugar

½ teaspoon cornflour

1 tablespoon stir-fry or
    sunflower oil

1 tablespoon fresh ginger,
    peeled and finely chopped

1 tablespoon garlic, peeled
    and finely chopped

500 g/1 lb lean boneless
    tender beef, cut into very
    thin strips

2 cups Chinese broccoli,
    cut into smallish pieces

225 g/ 8 oz mangetout

½ green pepper, deseeded
    and cut into fine strips

Combine the soy sauce, sherry, sugar and cornflour in a bowl. Heat a wok or a large frying pan over a moderately high heat and add the oil. When very hot, add the ginger and garlic and stir-fry for 30 seconds. Next add the beef and stir-fry for about 2 minutes until well browned. Now add the vegetables and stir-fry for about 3 minutes until everything is well combined and aromatic. Stir the soy sauce mixture and add it to the wok. Bring to the boil, tossing and stirring until thickened and smooth.

Serve immediately with rice or noodles.

Steaks with Brandy Cream Sauce

I enjoy a fillet steak cooked rare, without anything getting in the way of the true taste of excellent beef. However, this dish is an exception, a truly perfect combination of texture and flavour. This is a Rick Stein recipe.

Serves 4

2 tablespoons olive oil
4 fillet steaks
50 g/2 oz butter
2 cloves of garlic, peeled
    and finely chopped
2 teaspoons Dijon mustard
2 tablespoons brandy
2 tablespoons water
salt and pepper
4 tablespoons cream

Heat the oil in the frying pan and add the steaks, cooking according to taste. Remove and keep warm. Add the butter to the pan and, when melted, add the garlic and sauté for 1 minute. Then add the mustard, stirring until smooth. Add the brandy, water and seasoning and stir until the sauce bubbles. Finally add the cream, reduce the heat and simmer for a minute more.

Serve steaks with sauce spooned over the top.

pork

Pigs have always been of extraordinary significance in Ireland. In ancient times Ireland was known as Muc Inis or Hog Island, Muc being Gaelic for 'pig'. According to legend, the Tuatha, a group who followed the goddess Danu, caused a fog to rise over the land with the appearance of a large pig, which caused it to be named Muc Inis.

In Tipperary the mountain ridge of Slievenamuck (which translates as 'Mountain of the Pigs') is the site of the legendary slaying of a wild sow called Beo, which had devastated much of Munster. Fionn was the hero who killed Beo with a set of spears forged especially for the task, so the hills were named accordingly.

Pork in Ireland

One of my fondest childhood food memories is a steaming serving of bacon and cabbage. I'm probably not alone in this. It is a meal that conjures up all that is comforting and delicious about home cooking. Of course the quality of the pork is fundamental and in Ireland we have a worldwide reputation for excellence in the sector.

Unlike many cultures where the pig has a negative connotation, in Ireland it is an animal that has always been central to the well-being of most rural families and is consequently very highly regarded. Unlike other animals, the pig was alone in being kept specifically for consumption. Pigs, being omnivores, could forage on whatever was available, and were therefore cheap to fatten for slaughter, living happily off scraps and whatever they could find in the forests.

Traditionally they were slaughtered in the autumn, after growing in the spring and fattening in the summer. A general rule was that a pig could be slaughtered only in months of the year with an 'r', since the meat would deteriorate in the summer months. Even today there is reduced demand for pork in these months, as traditionalists follow the message of their childhood, often without realising why.

In times past, the slaughtering of the pig was regarded as men's business, the curing and salting the responsibility of women. Most of the meat would be cured, with the parts of the carcass not suited to preservation kept back as fresh pork and enjoyed and shared with neighbours in what was called a 'pig round'. Different cuts would be assigned according to occupation, with the butcher who killed the beast being given the neck.

No part of the animal would be wasted and even the blood was used as the basis of black pudding, an essential part of any Irish breakfast. The intestines were kept back for use as casings and cut into lengths tied at one end. Every farmer had his own mix, but it consisted basically of the collected blood of the slaughtered pig and additions of oatmeal, spices when available, salt, lard and onions. The preparation of black pudding in the home continued into the mid-twentieth century before it was widely produced on a commercial basis.

White pudding was traditionally made from the remaining offal of the pig, with the addition of lard, spices and cereal, the omission of pig's blood altering the taste significantly.

Brawn has always been appreciated for its unique and delicious qualities, and each farmer's wife had her own way of creating it. The head was boiled to a jelly along with the tail, and sometimes the tongue; the meat removed, finely chopped and flavoured with pepper, allspice and nutmeg. This was pressed into a container, covered with a weight and left to set.

Crubeens or pigs' trotters are another Irish delicacy, traditionally a teatime or supper food that many would describe as an acquired taste. Pigs' trotters have been enjoyed along with a pint of stout in many an Irish pub in times past and are a well-established part of the Irish culinary story. The front trotters are regarded as the most satisfying succulent meat to suck on and I have to say they are one of my favourite foods. There was many an evening's journey to 'Imelda's Chipper' when I was growing up, with the longest queue in Clonmel testament to the band of hungry fans. The shop opened at 9.00 p.m. and closed at midnight and we waited with mounting anticipation for Imelda to open the doors for our order. Crubeens and chips were the Clonmel equivalent to fish and chips in popularity and any occasion for a feed was a treat. My Aunt Lena was a dab hand at cooking them to perfection and a proposed visit to her house would guarantee an enthusiastic response from us.

Crubeens could not be easier to cook and, as with so many traditional recipes, the key is to cook them for as long as it takes until the meat falls off the bone, probably two to three hours. Just cover the trotters with water in a large saucepan, add a carrot, some parsley, a large onion and a few peppercorns and simmer.

The sight of salted meat hanging from the rafters must have been a fond one for many an Irish family of the past, with the knowledge that a tasty feed was always on hand, no matter the weather or time of year. Smoked bacon could be kept for months, developing unique flavours during the process. Despite refrigeration being the obvious means of storing meat today, there are many in Ireland who would prefer the saltiness of cured salted bacon as enjoyed by families decades ago. There are a few traditional butchers who still hang the white salted bacon in their shops and it is a hope of mine that these artisans continue with their craft.

What about Pork?

Good-quality pork is meat that is firm and pink, showing no trace of moisture. It is considered to be a white meat, but in nutritional terms is grouped with red meat. Current trends demand that pigs provide more meat than past breeds, and are now slaughtered at six or seven months, weighing somewhere between 90 and 100 kg. Because the meat is leaner today, pork is generally regarded as less tasty than in the past. It is an unfortunate fact that quality and flavour have suffered in the chase for leaner meat and faster-maturing pigs.

Pork is not hung: good pork is fresh pork and that is just how it should look – with a slight shine. The fat should be creamy and the meat pink. Free-range and organic pork will be slightly darker in colour.

A guilty pleasure for many is the pork crackling from a roast and it can be the highlight of the meal when cooked to perfection. Just the sight of that golden coat on the loin of pork just out of the oven and the aromas of roasted meat would get the hunger pangs going. While many would declare it a favourite food, the diet-conscious would be horrified. The solution to satisfy all tastes is to lift the crackling from the meat after it is cooked, leaving it to the gourmands to tackle it among themselves!

Pork fat lies just beneath the surface of the pig and at one time was a staple item for chefs and diners alike. Pork belly fat consists of muscular tissue streaked with fat and can be cured or smoked for excellent bacon rashers.

Although pork has traditionally been a rich and fatty meat, current concerns regarding fat content have dictated that pigs be reared with a minimum of fat cover. The resulting loss of flavour means that most pork benefits from being cooked with the addition of aromatic herbs and spices and enlivened with flavoursome vegetables and fruit such as apples and prunes.

Rashers are a daily fix for those who enjoy the 'full Irish breakfast' made up of bacon rashers, black pudding (blood sausages), pork sausages and an egg on the side; the highlight of the day for many, either on a plate or all piled together in a roll. The demand for cured bacon is considerable in Ireland and across the world, and the enormous scale of

the bacon industry feeding this demand has led to shortcuts to maximise profit. Intensive farming methods and fast-tracking of the curing process mean that the consumer often pays the price in bland-tasting and poorly textured pork.

Industrial bacon is injected with basic brine, made up mostly of salt and sugar, or by immersing it in brine for a short time. The maturing process has been reduced to just a few hours, with no time being given to allow the meat to 'cure'. Insufficient time is allowed for the bacon to drip out the excess moisture and bagging it too quickly results in too much water still left in the product. Sadly, when producing for the mass market it can be all about speed and haste. Time is vital in the process of meat production and it is the factor that costs money in any business. Bypassing this crucial element compromises the quality of the product and the consumer is cheated of the true taste as it should be. The food industry has even developed an 'instant cure', where water is added to a special powder mix to create a paste, which shortens the process considerably. The resulting manufactured taste is homogenised and bland and, sadly, it is what the consumer is buying from most supermarket shelves. The very nature of the curing process means that it should never be associated with the word 'instant'.

Ham and bacon produced for the mass market also contain more liquid than the traditional dry-cured product, often containing more weight in moisture than the original raw meat. The evidence always turns up in the cooking process. If you find yourself with a spitting, curling rasher that leaches liquid into your pan, you have an industrially processed and, in my opinion, inadequate piece of meat. Once cooked, the rasher is about a third of its raw weight. It really is false economy when you consider that the cost is calculated by weight.

We stock pork and bacon products only from passionate artisan pork and bacon producers located locally. Our pork comes from a family-owned business with generations of expertise brought to all aspects of the process. Sowing the seeds for food crops, harvesting the corn, barley and wheat and milling and manufacturing the feed mean that there is total quality control in the fattening process of their stock.

The commitment to best practice continues through the breeding and slaughtering of their animals, and finally processing into the superb product they provide for us. This complete integration of production of pork from seed to the end of the chain is very unusual.

The smoked ham and bacon supplied to us is unique because it has been smoked on racks in a smokehouse over beechwood chips, resulting in a complexity of aromas and taste that is simply superb. The hams are hung in the smokehouse for 3½ hours, then

taken out and let rest for twenty-four hours to cool down before being ready for the plate.

The artisan butcher, seeking to provide only the best for his customers, will use only bacon and pork that meet the criteria he or she has set. For most butchers who stand outside the sweep of the giant supermarket offerings, this means partnering with dedicated producers who stand behind the quality of their locally bred, locally reared and locally prepared pigs. For this reason seek out a good independent butcher and banish those limp, sad, curled-up rashers forever.

Which cuts?

There are fewer primal cuts in pork because the loin and rib are dealt with as one piece. Loin chops can be the most expensive, as they are quick to cook. The same principle applies as in all animals: the cuts with more muscle require longer, slower cooking than the prime cuts.

Pork recipes

As a boy, part of the school holidays was always spent at my father's home place with my grandmother. It was a farm in the neighbouring county and, while we grew up around animals and meat and enjoyed a familial farming heritage, effectively we were raised in the heart of a town. During the holidays spent with my grandmother one particular job I loved was when my sister and I would take a jug to the tank where the milk was chilled and waiting for collection, and skim the cream off the top. My grandmother would have the potatoes ready, hot and piled in a dish and we would pour the cream over them, add butter and top with salt. Food heaven and what could be better? It is this simple food I have always enjoyed the most, with the individual quality of each ingredient making it outstanding.

My grandmother's bacon and cabbage was another memorable experience, and was just how her mother prepared it before her. The combination of home-reared meat and floury potatoes make my grandmother's bacon and cabbage the one I have always maintained is the best I've ever tasted.

Given how bacon and cabbage is thought of as such a traditional dish, it is often disregarded as being uninteresting. I urge you to revisit it – you'll be pleasantly surprised.

Traditional Bacon and Cabbage with Parsley Sauce

Bacon and cabbage, as a dish, is the original Irish comfort food and evokes memories for many on the island. The only accompaniment needed is a pot of floury potatoes.

Serves 6

1.5 kg/3 lb loin of bacon
1 medium carrot, peeled
    and chopped
2 celery stalks, sliced
2 leeks, sliced
1 teaspoon peppercorns
1 cabbage, trimmed and
    cut into quarters

Parsley Sauce
50 g/2 oz butter
50 g/2 oz plain flour
570 ml/20 fl oz milk (or half
    milk/half cooking liquid)
cup parsley, chopped
salt and pepper

Place the joint in a large saucepan, add the vegetables and peppercorns, cover with cold water and bring to the boil. Simmer gently for approximately 20 minutes per 500 g/1 lb plus 20 minutes extra. When the bacon is cooked, remove it from the pot to rest while the cabbage is cooking. Scoop out the vegetables from the liquid and add the cabbage, simmering it for 15 minutes, then drain and reserve the liquid.

To make the parsley sauce, melt the butter in a saucepan and add the flour. Cook, stirring, for a few minutes. Whisk in the milk and bring the sauce to the boil. Reduce the heat and simmer for 3–4 minutes. Add the parsley and taste for seasoning. Keep warm.

Slice the bacon and serve with the cabbage and potatoes, with the sauce to pour over the meat.

If you want to move away from the traditional and make this a little more luxurious, try cooking it in cider instead of water.

Warm Black Pudding and Bacon Salad

Adding black pudding to this salad results in a substantial dish that is really quick to prepare and ideal for a summer lunch. It's an innovative way to transform black pudding from a simple breakfast staple.

Serves 6

2 tablespoons olive oil
6 potatoes, peeled, boiled and chopped into
    1.25 cm/½ inch dice
85 g/3 oz back bacon, chopped
110 g/4 oz black pudding, chopped into
    1.25 cm/½ inch dice
mixed salad leaves

Dressing
2 tablespoons olive oil
1 tablespoon grainy mustard
1 tablespoon white wine vinegar

Heat the olive oil in a large frying pan. Add the potatoes, bacon and black pudding and sauté for 5 minutes.

Meanwhile place the salad greens in a large bowl and prepare the dressing. In a small bowl whisk together the olive oil, mustard and white wine vinegar. When the potatoes, bacon and black pudding have cooked through, add them to the bowl of salad and toss through the dressing. Serve immediately.

Lina's Brawn

My wife has Lithuanian heritage and has introduced me to a whole new world of flavours, meats, vegetables and cooking methods. Brawn is enjoyed in all countries with a strong rural background, since no part of an animal would be wasted. This recipe is adapted from an eastern European version which, I believe, adds an interesting twist.

Serves 6

3 crubeens (preferably
    already cooked)
1 ham shank (preferably
    already cooked)
2 chicken legs
500 g/1 lb corned beef, cut
    into 2.5 cm/1 inch cubes
2 medium carrots, peeled
    and chopped
1 medium onion, peeled
    and chopped
2 cloves of garlic, peeled
    and chopped
1 bay leaf
5 black peppercorns

Put everything into a big saucepan and cover it with water. Bring to the boil and simmer for about 1½ hours. (If you do not have a cooked ham shank or crubeens, you will have to cook them first for three hours and then add the remaining meat.)

After it is cooked, the meat should come away from the bone quite easily. Chop all the meat finely. Drain the liquid and set it aside. Put the chopped meat back in the saucepan and add enough cooking liquid just to cover the meat. (Too much liquid will make the brawn very gelatinous.) Bring it to the boil and simmer for a few minutes. Pour the mixture into a loaf tin or terrine and leave it to cool. Once cool, put it into the fridge to set. Serve sliced.

Bacon and Cabbage with Mustard Crust

This is effectively traditionally cooked bacon but finished off in the oven with the addition of a crumbed topping. It lifts the everyday bacon dish to a higher level.

Serves 6

1.5 kg/3 lb loin of bacon

1 medium carrot, peeled
and chopped

2 celery stalks, chopped

2 leeks, sliced

1 teaspoon peppercorns

1 cabbage, trimmed and
finely sliced

butter to dress cabbage
(optional)

Breadcrumb Topping

1 tablespoon dry or wet
mustard

1 tablespoon oven-dried
breadcrumbs

½ tablespoon brown sugar

50 g/2 oz softened butter

Mustard Sauce

50 g/2 oz butter

30 g/1 oz plain flour

1 tablespoon dry mustard

150 ml/5 fl oz cooking liquid

150 ml/5 fl oz cream

salt and pepper

Place the bacon in a large saucepan. Add the chopped vegetables and peppercorns and cover with cold water. Bring to the boil, reduce the heat and simmer gently for approximately 20 minutes per 500 g/1 lb.

Preheat the oven to 200°C/400°F/gas mark 6. When the joint is cooked, remove it from the saucepan, reserving the liquid. Remove the rind from the bacon and score the fat by cutting through with the tip of a very sharp knife. Combine all the ingredients for the breadcrumb topping in a small bowl to create a paste. Spread the joint with the topping, put it in a roasting dish and roast for 15–20 minutes.

To make the mustard sauce, melt the butter and add the flour and mustard. Cook for a minute or two. Whisk in the cooking liquid and cream. Bring to the boil. Reduce the heat and simmer for 3–4 minutes and taste for seasoning. The sauce should have the consistency of thin cream. Keep warm.

Bring the cooking liquid to the boil, add the cabbage, and simmer for 15 minutes or so. Drain and toss with a little butter if desired. Slice the bacon and serve on the bed of cabbage, a little of the mustard sauce and, of course, floury potatoes.

Corn and Bacon Chowder

This is a hearty and satisfying dish, ideal for a weekend brunch or as a supper dish.

Serves 6

2 medium onions, peeled
    and finely chopped
1 tablespoon olive oil
50 g/2 oz plain flour
1 teaspoon turmeric
4 cups chicken stock
2 large potatoes, peeled
    and chopped into
    1.25 cm/½ inch dice
250 g/9 oz Cheddar cheese,
    cut into 1.25 cm/½ inch
    dice
2 cups milk
4 bacon rashers, cut into
1.25 cm/½ inch dice
    and fried
1 cup corn kernels, fresh
    or canned
salt and pepper
parsley, finely chopped,
    to garnish

Fry the onions in the oil and cook until aromatic and soft, but not brown. Add the flour and turmeric and stir into the onion mix. Add 1 cup of the stock and blend with the onion mixture. Pour it all into a large saucepan. Add the rest of the stock and the potatoes and simmer until the potatoes are cooked.

Add the cheese, milk, bacon and corn and simmer until the cheese has melted. Season to taste and serve sprinkled with fresh parsley.

Pork and Pistachio Terrine

When plated up and garnished this terrine looks as good as it tastes; it's ideal for a picnic or as part of a summer buffet spread.

Serves 8

700 g/1½ lb lean pork
250 g/9 oz pork belly
250 g/9 oz chicken livers, trimmed
110 g/4 oz streaky bacon rashers
1 teaspoon salt
½ teaspoon black pepper
3 tablespoons brandy
butter to grease terrine dish
2 shallots, peeled and finely chopped
1 egg, beaten
110 g/4 oz pistachio nuts
bay leaves to cover base of terrine
8 thinly sliced bacon rashers

Preheat the oven to 180°C/350°F/gas mark 4.

Put all the meat into a food processor and blend until it is finely chopped. Empty the minced meat into a large bowl and add seasoning and brandy. Mix together and leave covered in the refrigerator for several hours.

Lightly butter a loaf tin or terrine. When ready to cook, add the shallots, egg and pistachios to the meat mixture and combine well.

Arrange enough bay leaves to cover the base of the terrine dish or loaf tin and line it with the bacon rashers, leaving enough hanging over the sides to complete the wrap of the filling. Spoon the filling into the terrine and then fold the bacon over the top. Cover the top with greaseproof paper and wrap the whole terrine in aluminium foil.

Half-fill a large baking dish with hot water. Place the terrine in the baking dish and cook for 1½ hours, until the meat is shrinking away from the sides of the terrine. Lift the cooked terrine from the water and cool in aluminium foil. Once cool, refrigerate. Serve sliced with crusty bread and salads.

Bacon and Egg Pie

Everyone loves a pie and the combination of bacon and egg is a winner. This is perfect picnic food and can be made the day before. The taste develops if it is served at room temperature.

Serves 6–8

1 quantity of shortcrust
  pastry (see page 246)
6 rashers thickly sliced
smoked streaky bacon
2 tablespoons parsley,
  finely chopped
1 teaspoon chives, finely
  chopped
12 eggs
125 g/4½ oz cream cheese
salt
freshly ground black pepper

Preheat the oven to 180°C/350°F/gas mark 4.

Line a 22 cm/9 inch loose-bottomed flan tin with just over half the pastry and chill for 30 minutes. Roll out the rest of the pastry to make a lid and set aside.

Lightly fry the bacon and cut into pieces. Scatter two-thirds of the bacon over the base of the pastry case. Scatter half the herbs on top of the bacon and then add 11 eggs carefully, one at a time, taking care not to break the yolks.

Season and add the rest of the herbs followed by the remaining bacon and the cream cheese cut into cubes. Cover with the pastry lid and let it settle over the hump of the eggs. Trim and seal carefully. Whisk the remaining egg with a pinch of salt and brush over pastry. Bake for 35 minutes until a rich golden colour. Allow to cool before removing from the tin. Serve warm or at room temperature.

Pea and Ham Soup

This hearty soup is the perfect way to use the ham bone after Christmas or bacon hocks from your butcher. Slow, long cooking renders the meaty bits to melt-in-the-mouth perfection.

Serves 6–8

50 g/2 oz butter

1 medium onion, peeled
and finely chopped

2 medium carrots, peeled
and chopped

2 large potatoes, peeled
and chopped

4 bacon rashers, chopped

175 g/6 oz green split dried
peas, washed and drained

1 ham bone

1 litre/35 fl oz water or ham
stock

3 sprigs mint, finely chopped

Melt the butter in a large saucepan and add the onion, carrots, potatoes and bacon and cook for 10 minutes or until the vegetables are soft. Add the split peas, ham bone and water or stock and simmer for at least 1 hour until the peas have softened to a paste.

Sprinkle over fresh mint to serve.

Pork Schnitzel

Schnitzel is originally a German dish and, by tradition, pork is hugely popular in Germany. The key to great schnitzel is definitely in the pounding of the pork. The flavours here are great and can be served with other German favourites such as apple sauce or red cabbage.

Serves 4

4 pork steaks

6 stale slices of bread, processed to breadcrumbs

1 tablespoon Gruyère cheese, finely grated

2 tablespoons parsley, finely chopped

1 egg, beaten

2 tablespoons olive oil

Trim the pork steaks of any fat and flatten them out by hammering lightly with a rolling pin or similar object. Mix the breadcrumbs, cheese and parsley together. Dip the pork steaks into the beaten egg and bathe in the breadcrumb mixture, pressing well to make sure they are completely covered.

Heat the oil in a large frying pan and fry the schnitzels for 4–5 minutes each side, until golden and cooked through.

Pork Spare Ribs

There is only one way to eat ribs and that is with your fingers. It's a messy business, so napkins and finger bowls are essential. The combination of sweet and spicy with fruity overtones turns a strip of ribs into a feast. The ribs should be marinated overnight for the best result.

Serves 4

1 cup soy sauce

¾ cup brown sugar

¼ cup balsamic vinegar

¼ cup tomato paste

¼ cup orange juice

2 tablespoons grainy
    mustard

1 teaspoon ground ginger

½ teaspoon ground
    cinnamon

½ teaspoon hot chilli powder

½ teaspoon cumin powder

pork spare ribs (allow 4 for
    each person)

Preheat the oven to 200°C/400°F/gas mark 6.

Combine all the ingredients except the pork and mix well. Heat in a saucepan, stirring constantly until it boils. Remove from the heat and allow to cool completely.

Lay the ribs in a flat dish, cover with the marinade and refrigerate for several hours minimum. Reserve any extra sauce.

Pour any remaining marinade over the ribs and bake for 45 minutes. Serve when cooled to room temperature.

Barbecued Marinated Pork Steaks

There's something very masculine about a barbecue. Maybe it's the idea of cooking outside but, whatever the reason, these pork steaks will go down a treat.

Serves 6

6 pork steaks

Marinade
zested rind of 2 oranges
½ cup orange juice
1 tablespoon Dijon mustard
2 teaspoons soy sauce
2 tablespoons white wine vinegar
1 tablespoon brown sugar
salt and pepper

Combine all the marinade ingredients in a bowl and stir well. Place the pork in a glass bowl and pour over half the marinade. Cover and refrigerate for several hours.

Drain the pork and chargrill or barbecue over a medium heat until cooked through, basting the steaks with the remaining marinade.

Chinese Pork Balls

Best-quality pork should be used for this recipe. Ask your butcher to mince it for you. Belly pork or shoulder will provide the fat content that will keep the result sweet and juicy.

Serves 6

500 g/1 lb pork,
    finely minced
1 shallot, peeled and
    finely chopped
2 cloves of garlic, peeled
    and finely chopped
¼ teaspoon ground ginger
2 tablespoons cornflour
1 teaspoon sherry
1 teaspoon salt
¼ teaspoon white pepper
oil for deep frying

Mix together all the ingredients except the oil and, with moistened hands, shape the pork into small balls, roughly the size of a walnut. Heat the oil in a deep fryer and fry the pork balls until browned. Lift out and drain on some kitchen paper.

Serve immediately with sweet and sour sauce or chilli sauce.

Pork and Beans

For real comfort food, this is hard to beat. All kinds of beans work superbly well with pork, and beans are highly nutritious.

Serves 6–8

500 g/1 lb dried haricot
   beans, soaked overnight
   in water and drained
500 g/1 lb salt pork
2 onions, peeled and
   chopped
3 tablespoons brown sugar
3 tablespoons dark treacle
2 teaspoons dry mustard
2 teaspoons salt
freshly ground black pepper
2 cups liquid from the beans
4 tablespoons tomato
   ketchup
1 teaspoon Worcestershire
   sauce

Preheat the oven to 150°C/300°F/gas mark 2.

Place the drained beans in a large saucepan and cover with water and bring to the boil. Cook for 1 hour or so. Strain and reserve the liquid.

Pour boiling water over the salt pork, then slash the rind with a sharp knife in several places. Cut the pork into two pieces and lay one piece in a large, deep casserole.

Mix together the onions, brown sugar, treacle, mustard, salt and pepper and 2 cups of the bean liquid. Place the beans on top of the pork and pour over the onion mixture. Stir and place the remaining pork on top, rind side up. Cover tightly and cook in the oven for 3½ hours or until the pork is tender. Add tomato and Worcestershire sauces mixed together and cook uncovered for a further 30 minutes. If the mixture is too dry, add more bean liquid.

Excellent served with pork sausages and mashed potatoes.

Rolled Herb Pork with Crackling

Pork combines well with herbs and this recipe is excellent served hot from the oven or cold from the fridge. It's a perfect choice as part of a picnic spread or party occasion.

Serves 6

olive oil to coat baking tray

4 cloves of garlic, peeled and finely chopped

2 tablespoons fennel seeds

2 tablespoons rosemary, finely chopped

2 tablespoons parsley, finely chopped

2 tablespoons chives, finely chopped

3 tablespoons olive oil

2 kg/4½ lb loin of pork, butterflied

salt

freshly ground black pepper

Preheat the oven to 220°C/425°F/gas mark 7.

Lightly coat a baking tray with olive oil.

Grind the garlic, fennel, herbs and olive oil to a paste with a pestle and mortar or herb grinder. Open the pork loin out and spread the paste over it. Roll the loin and secure with string tied at intervals to keep the pork secured during cooking. Sprinkle a little salt over the pork and place on the baking tray. Cook in the oven for 20 minutes or so until the skin is crisp and browned.

Reduce the heat to 180°C/350°F/gas mark 4 and cook the pork for a further 2 hours. When it is cooked, remove the pork from the oven and cover with aluminium foil. Allow it to stand covered for at least 10 minutes before carving.

For an easy side dish, place scrubbed jacket potatoes in the oven for the last hour of cooking and fill with garlic butter or grated cheese. A fresh green salad makes an ideal side dish.

Bacon and Mushroom Pasta

This is a super-quick supper dish that I often make in the autumn when the mushrooms pop up across the fields of our farm. While picking wild mushrooms, make sure you know what you're doing, since some mushrooms are not what they seem. If in any doubt, just buy some.

Serves 6

500 g/1 lb pasta
salt
2 tablespoons olive oil
1 medium onion, peeled
    and finely chopped
2 cloves of garlic, peeled
    and finely chopped
10 slices dry-cured smoked
    bacon, chopped
2 cups mushrooms,
    cleaned and sliced
½ cup cream
pepper
125 g/4½ oz Parmesan
    cheese, grated

Cook the pasta in plenty of salted water according to the instructions.

Heat the oil in a large pan and add the onion, cooking for several minutes until aromatic. Add the garlic and mix. Remove from the pan on to a paper towel. Cook the bacon in the pan until brown and add the mushrooms. Return the onions to the pan at the same time. Cook for a further few minutes until the mushrooms start to wilt. Add the cream, season to taste and combine the pan contents with the cooked, drained pasta.

Serve sprinkled with grated Parmesan.

Sausage Rolls

These sausage rolls are legendary and as popular in Ireland as they are in Australia where the recipe originated. Make double or even triple the quantity because the crowd will keep coming back for more.

Makes 48

2 packets frozen puff pastry
500 g/1 lb sausages or
    sausage meat
2 cups grated carrots
2 cups onion, peeled and
    finely chopped
2 cups potato, peeled
    and grated
2 cups parsley, finely
    chopped
¼ cup tomato ketchup
salt and pepper
2 eggs, beaten

Preheat the oven to 180°C/350°F/gas mark 4.

Defrost the pastry and cut each square in half. Roll out the pastry to 5 mm/½ inch thick. De-skin the sausages, if used, by soaking in cold water for 10 minutes and then slipping off the casings.

Combine the sausage meat, vegetables, parsley sauce, tomato sauce and seasoning in a large bowl and mix thoroughly. Place a 'tunnel' of sausage mix in the centre of the pastry strip. Brush the edges with the egg wash and roll up so that the edges just overlap.

Place the long rolls onto an oiled baking tray, nudging each other so that there is no space between. Brush the tops with egg and cut across the roll with a sharp knife to the length desired.

Bake for about an hour or until the sausage rolls are golden and cooked through.

Pork Filo Pie

Filo pastry is easy to use and readily available. Because of the nature of the sheets of pastry, care must be taken to make sure that they are kept whole.

Serves 6

500 g/1 lb lean pork mince

1 pork steak/fillet, minced in a food processor

1 egg, beaten

1 cup feta cheese, crumbled

½ cup parsley, finely chopped

½ cup fresh coriander, finely chopped

2 tablespoons mint, finely chopped

1 teaspoon dried chilli (optional)

½ teaspoon ground cumin

salt and pepper

finely grated zest of a lemon

10 tablespoons melted butter or olive oil

10 sheets filo pastry

Preheat the oven to 220°C/425°F/gas mark 7.

Place all the ingredients, except the pastry and butter or oil, into a large bowl and mix well.

Lightly brush a baking dish with butter or oil and carefully peel a layer of the filo pastry. Lay one sheet at a time in the dish, leaving some pastry hanging over the edge. Brush each sheet with the melted butter or oil, repeating the process until 5 sheets have been used. Spoon in the pork mixture and lay the remaining sheets on top, brushing each with butter or oil. Glaze the top with any remaining butter or oil and ensure that the pie is sealed at the edges. Bake in the oven for 40 minutes.

This is particularly good served with potato salad and a mix of green salad leaves.

Cider-glazed Ham

A glazed ham can be an eye-catching centrepiece for any occasion and is an easy option for maximum impact. The quality of the ham and the aromatic complexity of the smoking process are fundamental to the success of the meat, with the glazing the finishing touch that is so visually appealing.

Serves 10

1 smoked ham
175 g/6 oz brown sugar
½ cup Dijon mustard
1½ cups apple cider
2 large cooking apples,
    peeled, cored and sliced
    thickly and sprinkled with
    1 tablespoon brown sugar

Preheat the oven to 220°C/425°F/gas mark 7.

Remove the skin from the ham, being careful to leave on the fat. Score the fat into diamond shapes and place in a large roasting pan. Mix the sugar and mustard into a paste and apply evenly over the surface of the ham. Pour half the cider into the base of the pan and bake the ham for 15 minutes. Reduce the oven temperature to 200°C/400°F/gas mark 6.

Remove the ham from the oven and pour over the remaining cider. Secure the apple rings with toothpicks decoratively on the surface of the ham. Cook for a further 10 minutes or so until the apples are lightly caramelised.

Cool before serving.

Lamb

Lamb in Ireland

Sheep are traditionally low-maintenance animals with the ability to prosper on marginal land. They are also the one animal that has escaped intensive farming. Due to the blessing of good soil, Tipperary grass is nutrient-rich and at any time of the year sheep can be seen dotted around the landscape, even clinging to the sides of mountains, happily self-sufficient and grazing freely. Indeed you will even find the odd farmer keeping sheep as an environmentally friendly lawnmower. The result is premium-quality meat; local lamb is greatly appreciated by our customers. There is a discernible variation in taste and texture between sheep grazed in mountainous regions or on lowland grass, with mountain lamb gaining favour in restaurants around the country.

However, lamb, for all its eating qualities and flavour, is not a particularly favoured meat in Ireland. Traditionally sheep were kept for wool and also, perhaps surprisingly to the modern generation, for milk. The animal was probably slaughtered for meat only when its days were numbered, with the associated strongly flavoured meat of very old mutton requiring long cooking in a pot, with root vegetables added to soak up the flavours. This simple dish is a traditional Irish stew, well known around the world as a classic Irish dish. The simplicity of the ingredients that make up this famously white stew belies the lusciousness of the finished dish. Lamb is the meat of choice today for Irish stew, with mutton sidelined as being too strong in flavour for today's taste.

What about lamb?

Lean, grass-fed lamb provides us with an impressive nutrient-dense food that contains all the essential amino acids in just the right proportions that our bodies require. Put simply, lamb meat contains all the essential proteins, vitamins and minerals necessary for good health.

Being a herbivorous animal, it is another rich source of CLA (conjugated linoleic acid). CLA is produced naturally from linoleic acid and bacteria present in the stomachs of grass-eating animals. It cannot be manufactured by the human body. It should be noted that the leanest cuts of lamb have an average of 70–80 mg of cholesterol per 85 g/ 3 oz serving. This compares well to skinless chicken breast with 70 mg, and makes lamb an excellent choice for diet-conscious diners.

Lamb has significantly less marbling than other meats, with most of the fat visible on the outside edges of the meat. Trimming this fat after cooking reduces saturated fats and, more importantly, protects the meat from drying out during the cooking process. Some of the fat melts during cooking and is absorbed into the meat, but this acts as a natural tenderiser and, as with all meats, adds significant flavour.

Lamb fat is not very flavourful except when really crispy. It does not have the same flavour benefits of pork or beef fat, so removing the fat totally before eating is recommended.

Burning lamb fat has a particular odour that many people associate with the flavour of lamb. This intensely 'muttony' smell is stronger on the nose than the flavour of the meat is to the taste buds, but it is this aroma that can deter people from eating it. It is a hard fat, meaning that it has a higher melting point than the fat of beef and pork. This heat intensity gives the fat a waxy texture which is quite different from beef and pork.

Young, well-reared lamb is pink rather than purplish red, which would indicate older meat. It should look bright and moist, and should not be sticky. Premium lamb has fat that looks waxy and white with a thin coating evident on the edge of the meat cut. The lamb bone, when seen from the end, should be moist and red in colour, and not porous looking.

Texel sheep

Our sheep of choice are Texel, originally from the island of Texel off the coast of Holland. These sheep were first imported into Ireland in 1964 and adapted easily to conditions here. The most outstanding quality of the Texel breed is its remarkable muscle development and leanness. Texels develop only a minor fat covering of the body and are usually composed of 60 per cent lean meat. It is the leanness of the meat and its tender, succulent qualities that make this breed of lamb the obvious choice for our business.

The sheep destined for our customers are reared locally, a matter of kilometres from our farm, and are brought to us to fatten and be prepared for slaughter. In accordance with demand, lamb is brought to market young, ideally at five to six months old. The meat is tender and the earthy, aromatic taste of lamb that is well reared and slaughtered is appreciated as being unique and delicious.

As with the beef that passes through our system, the lamb is individually prepared for slaughter and maturing. One person is responsible for the process and takes pride in the quality of the outcome. In larger-scale abattoirs the meat is sprayed with water for cleaning, resulting in soggy, flabby fat cover. Our artisan approach means that the carcass is cleaned individually, which is slower and more labour intensive. However, the results make the effort well worth it, since the fat cover is firm and white, protecting the meat and allowing it to mature naturally.

Which cuts?

Lamb is cut into two sides and each side is then cut into three main primal cuts: fore-end, full loin and leg. The fore-end is the section from the fourth rib, including the neck. The shoulder is traditionally regarded as a fatty inferior cut, suitable for stewing. However, I have noticed it being elevated by chefs and cooks in recent times to providing superb 'melt-in-the-mouth' meat when roasted long and slow. The back gigot is cut into chops suitable for stewing.

The full loin is taken from the fourth rib to the leg and is cut into two pieces. The top piece with the ribs is called the 'fair' end, which can be cut into cutlets or roasted as a rack of lamb. The rest of the loin is usually cut into chops.

The leg is excellent as a roast, with the shank a popular cut for braising. The leg can be boned, or 'butterflied', and is a very good option for barbecuing. The meat from the leg, when diced, is used for casseroles, curries and kebabs.

Sheep have always provided essential sustenance, but the price paid by poor, hungry folk who were tempted to steal an animal was often extreme. A list of named felons transported to Australia, as recorded in the *Limerick Chronicle* on 29 June 1850, includes that of one William Hickey, sentenced to seven years' transportation for stealing a lamb from Sarah Nash.

Lamb recipes

Our mental associations with certain words can be very powerful indeed. Some associations are so ingrained in the subconscious that we don't even notice them as triggers for others. It is hard to think of strawberries without cream and I find it difficult to mention the word 'spring' without automatically moving on to 'lamb'. You just can't beat the thought of an Easter Sunday lunch with a nice leg of spring lamb.

I often think Easter is a much underestimated holiday. Easter occurs when the temperatures are on the up and new life is all around us. Unlike the prospect of a bleak January after the Christmas festivities, following Easter spring continues to unfold its

wonderment like a beautiful appetiser to summer and, being Irish, regardless of statistics and weather records we have an inbuilt, unerring 'hope gene' that always insists we look forward to a 'great' summer.

Talking of simplicity, I can't think of anything more elegantly simple, succulent and tasty than spring lamb. With major advances in animal husbandry, lamb is now available year round, but high demand is still intrinsically linked with springtime. As those who grew up with the tradition of lamb at Easter get older, the high demand in spring may wane. It is something that natural farmers of the future will have to tackle. At the moment, however, thankfully spring is still synonymous with lamb.

Rack of Lamb with Black Pudding and Red Wine Jus

This recipe is very easy to prepare and yet would sit well on any restaurant menu. The black pudding and potato cake combination is a winner.

Serves 4

2 racks of lamb, trimmed
salt and freshly ground
    pepper
2–3 tablespoons olive oil
4 sprigs of rosemary
    to garnish

Jus
125 ml/4 fl oz red wine
1 heaped tablespoon
    redcurrant jelly
1 teaspoon rosemary,
    chopped

Potato Cakes
150 g/5 oz black pudding
1 teaspoon Dijon mustard
300 g/10 oz creamy
    mashed potato
2–3 tablespoons sunflower oil

Preheat the oven to 180°C/350°F/gas mark 4.

First make the potato cakes. Cut the black pudding into three even-sized pieces and bake in the oven on a small baking tray for 6–7 minutes until cooked. Mix the black pudding, Dijon mustard and mashed potato together until evenly combined. Check for seasoning. Divide the mixture into four balls and shape each ball into a round cake.

Heat the sunflower oil in a non-stick frying pan and fry the cakes on both sides until golden. Place the potato cakes on a small baking tray and pop into the oven for 5 minutes to heat through before serving.

Using a sharp knife, divide each rack of lamb in two pieces. Season the lamb with salt and pepper. Heat the olive oil in a frying pan. Put the lamb in the pan and seal it for about 2 minutes on each side (1 minute for smaller joints). Transfer the lamb to a roasting tin and put it in the oven for about 10 minutes for medium and 15 minutes for well done.

When the lamb is cooked to your liking, remove it from the oven, cover it with aluminium foil and allow it to rest in a warm place for about 5 minutes. This gives the meat time to relax.

For the jus, put the wine, redcurrant jelly and rosemary in a small saucepan and bring to the boil. Simmer for 3–4 minutes until the mixture starts to reduce. Remove from the heat.

To serve, put a potato cake in the centre of each warm plate. Place the lamb on top of each potato cake and drizzle with red wine jus. Garnish with a sprig of rosemary.

Navarin of Lamb

Spring lamb and an abundance of seasonal vegetables make this a hearty dish that is easy to assemble. It is a nutritious, comforting stew and particularly good with crusty bread to mop up the juice.

Serves 6

- 1.5 kg/3 lb shoulder of lamb, boned
- 2 tablespoons plain flour seasoned with salt and pepper
- 1 tablespoon butter
- 1 tablespoon olive oil
- 1 teaspoon sugar
- 1 medium onion, peeled and quartered

- 2 celery stalks, chopped
- 3 cloves of garlic, peeled and crushed
- 1 teaspoon dried thyme
- 1 bay leaf
- 3 tablespoons tomato paste
- 500 ml/18 fl oz beef, lamb or vegetable stock
- 1 turnip, peeled and sliced

- 8 small onions, peeled
- 8 small potatoes, peeled
- 2 medium carrots, peeled and chopped
- 300 g/10 oz French beans
- 1 cup shelled peas
- salt and freshly ground black pepper
- 2 tablespoons parsley, finely chopped

Preheat the oven to 150°C/300°F/gas mark 2. Trim any excess fat from the meat and cut it into small chunks. Toss the meat in the seasoned flour. Heat the butter and oil in a heavy-based pan. Fry the meat in batches until golden brown and sprinkle with the sugar. Remove the batches of meat with a slotted spoon to a casserole dish.

When all the meat has been cooked, add the onion and celery to the frying pan and cook for a further 5 minutes or so. Stir in the garlic, thyme, bay leaf, tomato paste and stock and bring to the boil. Pour over the meat in the casserole. Add the turnip to the casserole, cover with a tight-fitting lid and bake in the oven for 1½ hours. Add the remaining vegetables and cook for a further hour or so until the meat is tender. Adjust the seasoning and scatter parsley over to serve.

Kashmiri Lamb Curry

Kashmir is in north India near the Himalayas. This spiced, slow-cooked lamb dish takes its name from that region. It is often found on menus in restaurants as Rogan Josh. While it is no doubt spicy, it was never intended to scorch the palate.

Serves 6

300 g/10 oz natural yoghurt

85 g/3 oz skinned almonds, chopped

2 teaspoons medium curry powder

2 teaspoons fresh ginger, peeled and finely chopped

3 cloves of garlic, peeled and finely chopped

1 teaspoon salt

1 kg/2 lb 4 oz lamb, diced into 2.5 cm/1 inch cubes

2 tablespoons sunflower oil

2 medium onions, peeled and finely chopped

2 bay leaves

1 green chilli, deseeded and finely chopped

juice of half a lemon

1 x 400 g/14 oz can of chopped tomatoes

300 ml/10 fl oz water

110 g/4 oz raisins

large handful of fresh coriander, chopped

In a large mixing bowl combine the yoghurt, almonds, curry powder, ginger, garlic and salt, stirring to mix well. Add the lamb to the yoghurt mixture, covering the meat well. (You could leave this to marinate in the fridge overnight or for a few hours before cooking.)

Heat the oil in a large saucepan and fry the onions with the bay leaves until golden brown, constantly moving them around the pan. Add the meat and yoghurt mixture to the pan and stir-fry for 5 minutes. Add the chilli, lemon juice and tomatoes to the mixture in the pan and stir-fry for another 5 minutes. Add the water, cover and leave to simmer over a gentle heat for 60 minutes. Add the raisins and most of the coriander and turn up the heat. Stir until the sauce has thickened.

Garnish with the remaining coriander and serve with rice.

Lamb Steaks with Rosemary

Lamb steaks are an excellent alternative to lamb chops for the barbecue. They are naturally meatier and benefit from marinating.

Serves 4

125 ml/4 fl oz dry white wine
2 cloves of garlic, peeled and crushed
¼ cup rosemary, coarsely chopped
¼ cup parsley, coarsely chopped
2 tablespoons soy sauce
1 tablespoon brown sugar
4 lamb steaks

Make a marinade by combining the wine, garlic, rosemary, parsley, soy sauce and brown sugar in a large bowl. Toss the lamb steaks in the mixture and cover and refrigerate for 3 hours or overnight.

Place the steaks under a hot grill or barbecue until browned. Cook as desired. Allow to relax in a warm place for 5 minutes before serving.

Roast Leg of Lamb with Lemon and Rosemary

Rosemary is a perfect match with the richness of lamb and the piquancy of the lemon is an excellent addition.

Serves 6–8

4 sprigs of rosemary
grated zest of 1 lemon
    (retain the flesh)
5 tablespoons olive oil
salt and freshly ground
    pepper
1.7–2 kg/3¾–4½ lb leg
    of lamb
1.2 kg/2½ lb new potatoes,
    scrubbed
8 cloves of garlic, unpeeled

Jus

150 ml/5 fl oz red wine
2 tablespoons redcurrant jelly
300 ml/10 fl oz beef or
    lamb stock

Preheat the oven to 230°C/450°F/gas mark 8.

Strip the leaves from half the rosemary and chop them. Mix with lemon zest into the olive oil. Season the lamb, smear with the olive oil and put in a roasting tin large enough to take the lamb and the potatoes. After 20 minutes reduce the oven to 200°C/400°F/gas mark 6. Baste the lamb and roast for 15 minutes per 500 g/1 lb for medium rare, 20 minutes for medium and 25 minutes for well done.

Forty-five minutes before the end of cooking put the potatoes, remaining rosemary and garlic around the lamb, basting them with the juices. Sprinkle with salt. Quarter the zested lemon and add this too. When the lamb is cooked, transfer it to a warm dish with the potatoes and leave to rest for 10 minutes in a warm place while you make the gravy.

Remove the rosemary and lemon from the roasting tin. Skim all but 3 tablespoons of fat from the tin. Squeeze the garlic cloves out of their skins into the tin. Put the tin over a low heat and add the wine to deglaze the pan, stirring to make sure all the crisp caramelised bits are mixed into the wine. Once the wine is bubbling, stir in the redcurrant jelly until well incorporated, then add the stock. Cook over a medium heat for 10–15 minutes until bubbling and slightly thickened. Strain into a warmed jug and serve with the meat.

Moussaka

Moussaka is a traditional Greek dish and you will find many varying recipes. This one is not difficult to prepare. Although it can be a little time-consuming, it is well worth the effort and always looks impressive when serving.

Serves 6

½ cup olive oil

1 kg/2 lb 4 oz lamb, minced

1 large onion, peeled and
    finely chopped

2 cloves of garlic, peeled
    and finely chopped

1 cup skinned and chopped
    tomatoes or 1 x 220 g/
    8 oz can of chopped
    tomatoes

2 tablespoons tomato paste

1 bay leaf

1 small onion, peeled and
    studded with 3 cloves

salt and pepper

1 teaspoon sugar

2 large aubergines

3 tablespoons plain flour

500 ml/18 fl oz white sauce
    (see page 238)

2 tablespoons Cheddar
    cheese

Preheat the oven to 180°C/350°F/gas mark 4.

Heat 2 tablespoons of olive oil in a heavy-based pan and add the meat. Cook for several minutes until browned and then add the onion and garlic. Continue to cook until the onion is soft. Add the tomatoes, tomato paste, bay leaf, clove-studded onion, seasoning, sugar and a half-cup of water. Cover and simmer for 30 minutes or so.

Cut the aubergines into slices and sprinkle with salt. Stand for 30 minutes to release the juices then wash, drain and pat dry. Dip the aubergine slices into the flour. Heat the remaining oil in a pan and add the aubergine. Fry until golden.

Arrange a layer of the aubergine slices over the base of a rectangular ovenproof dish and top with half the meat mixture. Repeat the layers, finishing with the aubergine slices.

Make up a batch of white sauce and stir in the cheese. Spread over the top of the dish as the final layer. Sprinkle with extra cheese if desired and bake for 30 minutes.

Apricot-stuffed Lamb

Shoulder of lamb has until recently been relegated to the 'too hard' basket, with most butchers dicing it for use in stews, casseroles and curries. Cooked long and slow on a low heat, this cut of meat is delicious, falling apart on the fork. For convenience, use canned apricots. Feel free to use fresh apricots if they're in season.

Serves 6

1.8 kg/4 lb shoulder of
   lamb, boned
salt and freshly ground
   black pepper
2 tablespoons olive oil
1 medium onion, peeled
   and sliced
1 medium carrot, peeled
   and sliced
1 bay leaf
300 ml/10 fl oz chicken stock

Stuffing

½ cup fresh white
   breadcrumbs
pinch of dried thyme
30 g/1 oz walnuts, chopped
1 small onion, peeled and
   chopped
1 tablespoon olive oil
1 x 213 g/7.5 oz can
   apricots, drained
salt and pepper
1 egg, beaten

Preheat the oven to 180°C/350°F/gas mark 4.

Season the lamb generously with salt and pepper and set aside while preparing the stuffing.

First make the stuffing. Place the breadcrumbs, thyme and walnuts in a bowl. In a small saucepan fry the onion in the oil until soft but not brown. This should take about 5 minutes. Add to the breadcrumb mixture. Chop the apricots coarsely and stir into the stuffing mixture. Season to taste and then bind with sufficient beaten egg to make a moist stuffing. Spoon the stuffing along the shoulder joint and tie with string into a long neat shape.

Heat the oil in a flameproof casserole and brown the meat on all sides. Add the sliced onion and carrot and the bay leaf. Pour over the stock and bring to the boil. Cover and cook in the oven for 2 hours or until well cooked and falling apart.

To serve, remove the string from the lamb and place on a serving dish. Sieve the stock juices and pour over the lamb. Carve into thick slices and serve.

Lamb Shank Soup

More a meal than a soup. While the vegetables on the list of ingredients are my favourites, add your own and make this a personal dish.

Serves 6–8

2 lamb shanks

2 medium onions, peeled
   and finely chopped

1 bay leaf

2 litres/3½ pints water

½ cup pearl barley

2 medium carrots, peeled
   and cut into 1.25 cm/
   ½ inch dice

2 leeks, sliced

2 celery stalks, finely sliced

2 potatoes, peeled and cut
   into 1.25 cm/½ inch dice

salt and pepper

2 tablespoons parsley,
   freshly chopped, to garnish

Put the shanks, onions and bay leaf into a large pot and add the water. Bring to simmering point and cook for 1 hour or so. Skim any scum from the top and add the rest of the ingredients, saving the parsley to sprinkle on the soup when serving. Cook for a further hour or until the shanks are tender.

Irish Stew

Irish stew isn't that Irish any more, with few of the younger generation making it to the traditional recipe. Made from lamb or mutton and potatoes, it is a flavoursome and filling comfort food which I believe is best eaten in winter. It is considered a white stew as opposed to the richer brown tones of a beef stew.

Serves 6

1 kg/2 lb 4 oz potatoes,
   peeled and sliced
2 large onions, peeled and
   sliced
5 tablespoons parsley,
   finely chopped
1 kg/2 lb 4 oz stewing lamb,
   cut into large pieces
1½ cups water
salt and freshly ground black
   pepper

Use a pot with a well-fitting lid and layer half the potatoes on the bottom. Then layer the onions, 3 tablespoons of the parsley and the meat, finishing with the potatoes. Pour over the water and add the seasoning. Cover and cook on a very low heat for 2½–3 hours until the meat is tender and the potatoes have broken into the liquid.

Serve sprinkled with the remaining chopped parsley and seasonings.

Lamb Kebabs

Ask your butcher to bone the lamb and cut it into decent-sized cubes for skewering. If you are using wooden skewers, it is always a good idea to soak them in water before using, since this will prevent them burning during cooking.

Serves 6

1.5 kg/3 lb leg of lamb,
    boned (butterflied)

Marinade

1 medium onion, peeled
    and sliced
2 cloves of garlic, peeled
    and crushed
salt
freshly ground black pepper
4 bay leaves, torn into pieces
1 teaspoon dried marjoram
2 tablespoons olive oil
½ cup dry white wine

Trim any excess fat from the lamb and cut into 2.5 cm/ 1 inch cubes if this hasn't already been done by your butcher. Put the meat in a bowl. In another dish combine the marinade ingredients and pour over the meat and mix well. Marinate overnight in the fridge and, when ready to grill, lift out the meat and thread on to skewers, with pieces separated by the bay leaves.

Heat the grill to red hot and place the skewered lamb under the heat and grill for 15–20 minutes, turning often and brushing with the marinade.

Roast Lamb with Herb Stuffing

Traditionally lamb heralds the arrival of spring, but these days lamb is available all year round. This is a great dish for an Easter Sunday feast.

Serves 6

1.5 kg/3 lb leg of lamb, boned (butterflied)
1 clove of garlic, peeled and cut into quarters
1 tablespoon olive oil
salt and pepper

Stuffing

handful of basil leaves, finely chopped
½ handful of parsley, finely chopped
3 streaky bacon rashers, finely chopped
3 cloves of garlic, peeled and finely chopped
freshly ground black pepper
2 tablespoons toasted pine nuts (dry cooked in oven for 10 minutes)

Preheat the oven to 200°C/400°F/gas mark 6.

Combine all the ingredients for the stuffing except the pine nuts and mix to a paste in a food processor or pestle and mortar. Add the pine nuts and mix.

With the tip of a sharp knife poke 4 incisions into the meat and insert the slivers of garlic. Rub the meat with the olive oil and season with salt and pepper.

Lay the lamb flat and layer with the stuffing mixture. Roll up and secure with string. Put the joint into a roasting pan and rub with a little olive oil. After 20 minutes reduce the heat to 180°C/350°F/gas mark 4. Cook for 1 hour for very rare lamb or 30 minutes extra for more well-done meat. Rest the lamb for 10 minutes covered with aluminium foil before slicing.

Persian Lamb Meatballs with Aubergine and Yoghurt Dip

I love it when life throws up a little culinary surprise and these meatballs are a perfect example of such treasures.

Serves 6

500 g/1 lb lamb, minced

1 medium onion, peeled
and finely chopped

2 teaspoons ground cumin

1 teaspoon ground
coriander

1 teaspoon freshly ground
black pepper

½ teaspoon salt

2 tablespoons raisins

2 tablespoons olive oil

Aubergine and yoghurt dip

1 large aubergine

2 cloves of garlic, peeled
and crushed

200 ml/7 fl oz Greek-style
yoghurt

1 tablespoon olive oil

1 teaspoon salt

½ teaspoon freshly ground
black pepper

½ cup fresh coriander,
finely chopped
(or parsley)

1 tablespoon lemon juice

To serve (optional)

pitta bread

1 medium red onion,
peeled and sliced

Preheat the oven to 180°C/350°F/gas mark 4.

To make the meatballs, combine all the ingredients except the oil and form into balls. I make them about golf-ball size and that seems to work pretty well. Heat the oil in a large pan and fry the meatballs until browned but still moist inside. Set aside and keep them warm.

To make the dip, prick the skin of the aubergine and bake in the oven for about 1 hour until very soft. When it is cool, remove the skin and place the pulp in a sieve and squeeze out the liquid. Place the mashed aubergine pulp in a bowl and add all the other ingredients and combine well. Refrigerate until ready to serve.

Traditionally the lamb meatballs and a dollop of the dip are placed on flat bread and rolled to enjoy as a wrap. The flat bread can be dry heated in a frying pan. Alternatively, heated pitta bread works well. Finely sliced red onion can be added if desired.

Pot-roasted Stuffed Shoulder of Lamb

The aromas that waft around the kitchen while a pot roast is cooking will make you want to prepare this lovely dish again and again.

Serves 6

1.5 kg/3 lb shoulder of
    lamb, boned
1 tablespoon plain flour
    seasoned with salt and
    freshly ground black
    pepper
1 tablespoon olive oil
1 medium onion, peeled
    and quartered

2 medium carrots, peeled
    and chopped
2 celery stalks, peeled and
    chopped
1 cup beef stock

Stuffing
2 streaky bacon rashers,
    chopped and fried in a
    little olive oil

½ cup fresh basil, torn into
    pieces
3 cloves of garlic, peeled
    and finely chopped
2 tablespoons parsley,
    finely chopped
1 cup fresh breadcrumbs
1 egg, beaten

To make the stuffing, combine all the ingredients, using enough beaten egg to bind the stuffing. Open out the shoulder and spread with the stuffing. Roll up and tie with string. Rub the seasoned flour into the shoulder.

Heat the oil in a cast iron or heavy-based pot. Brown the meat well on all sides over a moderate heat. Lift out the meat and put aside. Add the onion, carrots and celery and cook until soft and aromatic. Add the stock and bring to the boil. Return the meat to the pot. Cover and simmer gently for 2½ hours or until the meat is tender.

Lift the meat on to a serving platter and remove the string. The sauce can be sieved and spooned over the lamb to serve.

Braised Lamb Shanks with Rosemary and Balsamic Vinegar

Lamb shanks are delicious cooked long and slow. My favourite recipe for lamb shanks was given to me by Tamsin Day-Lewis, one of the world's favourite food writers and cooks. She has very kindly given me permission to share her best-loved recipe in this book.

Serves 4

2 tablespoons plain flour seasoned with sea salt and black pepper

4 lamb shanks

2–3 tablespoons olive oil, and possibly more

1 tablespoon rosemary leaves, finely chopped

1 dessertspoon thyme leaves, finely chopped

2 large onions, peeled and sliced thinly

6 cloves of garlic, peeled and roughly chopped

300 ml/10 fl oz white wine

150 ml/5 fl oz balsamic vinegar

bouquet garni of 2 strips of orange peel and 2 bay leaves tied together

Put the seasoned flour into a plastic bag and add the shanks, shaking to coat them evenly.

Heat the oil in a large, heavy-based casserole and brown the shanks on all sides over a medium heat. This should be done quickly – just a few minutes each side – until they begin to brown and crust. Scrape up any burnt bits of flour and remove with a slotted spoon. The pan may need more oil at this point. Add the rosemary and let it fizz. Then add the thyme, onions and garlic, stirring and cooking until the onions are softened and beginning to become transparent. Raise the heat and add the wine and vinegar, boiling for a few minutes.

Return the shanks and their juice to the pot. Lower the heat and add the bouquet garni tucked into the side. Cover the pot with a layer of greaseproof paper and put the lid on top. Simmer very gently for 2–2½ hours, turning the shanks occasionally.

Serve with champ (see page 212).

Poached Leg of Lamb on White Bean and Garlic Purée

The broth produced while cooking this recipe is alone worth the work involved; the lamb itself is always a taste sensation.

Serves 6

1.5 kg/3 lb leg of lamb, boned (butterflied) and bones reserved

2 tablespoons olive oil

2 medium onions, peeled and roughly chopped

1 medium carrot, peeled and chopped into 3 pieces

4 sprigs of parsley, finely chopped

4 sprigs of thyme to garnish

Seasoning

1 clove of garlic, peeled and finely chopped

2 sprigs of thyme

2 sprigs of rosemary, leaves chopped finely

salt and pepper

Combine seasoning ingredients and mix well. Fill the lamb cavity with the seasoning and roll, securing with string or skewers.

Cooking time for lamb should be around 15 minutes for every 500 g/1 lb. Heat the oil in a large pan, add the lamb bones and, over a high heat, ensure that they are heated on all sides. Remove any excess fat from the pan and add the onions, carrot and parsley to the bones and then add the rolled lamb. Cover the lamb with water and poach on a low heat for the calculated time. Make sure the lid of the pan is firmly on.

To make the purée, combine the beans, cream, garlic, rosemary and seasoning and cook, covered, for 5 minutes or so. Purée in a food processor and set aside.

When the lamb is cooked, remove from the pot and rest in a warm place. Strain the liquid and return it to the saucepan, boiling rapidly for 20 minutes to reduce it. Add any juices that drain from the resting meat.

Poached Leg of Lamb cont'd.

Bean and garlic purée

1 x 400 g/14 oz can of
    butter beans
1 cup cream
2 cloves of garlic, peeled
    and crushed
2 tablespoons fresh
    rosemary, finely chopped
salt and pepper

To serve, spoon the bean mix on to a plate and arrange sliced lamb on top. Moisten the lamb with a spoonful of the stock, and garnish with sprigs of fresh thyme.

Crumbed Lamb Cutlets

Crumbing or breadcrumbing is a really simple way to add flavour and crunch to an ordinary meal. It also bulks up the meat somewhat, making for a much more satisfying dish.

Serves 4

8 lamb cutlets
juice of half a lemon
salt and pepper
2 tablespoons plain flour
1 egg beaten with
    1 tablespoon water
1 cup fresh breadcrumbs
olive oil for frying

Trim the skin and excess fat from the lamb. Flatten with a rolling pin. Lay the cutlets on a plate and sprinkle with a little lemon juice. Season with salt and pepper. Coat the cutlets with the flour and then dip them into the beaten egg mix. Press the cutlets into the breadcrumbs and stand in the refrigerator for 30 minutes or so to set.

Heat the oil in a heavy frying pan and fry the cutlets for 5 minutes on either side. Lift them out, drain on kitchen paper and serve immediately.

Variations: Add 2 tablespoons of chopped parsley or grated Parmesan cheese to the breadcrumbs.

Lamb and Potato Pie

This is a pie with a unique taste and flavour. There is a little more work than usual in the preparation, but the result is worth it every time.

Serves 6

1 quantity shortcrust pastry
(see page 246)
3 tablespoons olive oil
1.5 kg/3 lb shoulder of lamb,
boned and cut into 2.5
cm/1 inch cubes
2 medium onions, peeled
and finely chopped
3 cloves of garlic, peeled
and finely chopped
2 tablespoons fresh rosemary,
chopped
1 x 400 g/14 oz can of
tomatoes
½ cup beef stock
¾ cup red wine
2 large potatoes, peeled, cut
into 2.5 cm/1 inch cubes
and cooked
2 sheets puff pastry
1 egg, lightly beaten

Preheat the oven to 220°C/425°F/gas mark 7.

Line a deep 25 cm/10 inch pie dish with the shortcrust pastry and refrigerate for at least 30 minutes.

Cover the pastry base with baking paper and fill with dried beans or other suitable blind baking materials and bake blind for 10 minutes. Remove beans and paper and return pie to the oven for a further 10 minutes or until a nice golden brown.

Heat the oil in a heavy-based saucepan or casserole dish and add the lamb in batches, cooking until browned all over. Remove to a warmed plate as you work. Add the onions and garlic to the pan and cook until the onions are soft. Add the rosemary and continue to cook for a few minutes. Return the meat to the pan and add the tomatoes, stock and wine. Cover and simmer for 1½ hours. Remove the lid and simmer for a further 30 minutes or until the lamb is tender. Add the potatoes and continue to simmer until the potatoes break down into liquid and the sauce has thickened. Set aside to cool.

Spoon the lamb mixture into the pastry case and cover with one sheet of puff pastry. Make shapes with the remaining pastry sheet to decorate the pie and brush with beaten egg. Place a ceramic pie vent in the centre of the dish to allow the steam to escape while cooking. If you have a proper pie vent to hand, stand it in the centre of the pastry base before spooning in the filling. If you don't have a pie vent, pierce the top of the pastry several times with a fork to create the necessary vents.

Bake at 220°C/425°F/gas mark 7 for 30 minutes or so until the pie is golden brown.

Barbecued Leg of Lamb

Barbecues are not just for steaks and sausages. Cooking a great big chunk of meat on a barbecue is every man's dream. Stoke up the coals and unleash the testosterone.

Serves 6

3 cloves of garlic, peeled and crushed to a purée with 1 teaspoon sea salt

2 tablespoons fresh thyme, chopped

2 tablespoons olive oil

grated zest of 1 lemon

2 tablespoons lemon juice

½ teaspoon freshly ground pepper

1.5 kg/3 lb leg of lamb, boned (butterflied)

Put the crushed garlic in a small bowl, add the thyme, oil, lemon zest, lemon juice and pepper and mix well. With the end of a sharp knife, pierce the skin of the lamb in 6 places. Rub the marinade over the lamb. Refrigerate for at least an hour.

Heat the barbecue grill or a griddle/chargrill pan. Place the lamb on the grill, skin side down, and cook for 15 minutes. Turn the lamb and cook for a further 15 minutes for medium or longer if desired. The lamb should be covered loosely with aluminium foil during the cooking process and left to stand away from the heat for 10 minutes before carving.

Spicy Lamb Meatballs

This is a quick but flavoursome meal. There is also something very gratifying about getting your hands dirty while forming the meatballs. The chilli is optional, so they don't have to be that spicy at all.

Serves 6

1 large potato, peeled and grated

1 large onion, peeled and grated

500 g/1 lb lamb, minced

4 cloves of garlic, peeled and finely chopped

1 red chilli, deseeded and finely chopped (optional)

salt and pepper

1 egg, beaten

1 cup fresh herbs such as parsley, coriander, tarragon and mint

1 teaspoon ground cinnamon

½ cup olive oil

Rinse the grated potato in cold water and with your hands squeeze out all the moisture. Place all the ingredients except the oil into a bowl and mix until well combined. Form the mixture into small balls and flatten them into pattie shapes. Heat the oil in a large pan and cook the meatballs in batches for about 5 minutes on each side, turning carefully.

Slow-roasted lamb

Cooking marinated meat for 6 hours may seem excessive, but the melt-in-the-mouth shredded meat that results makes it all worth while.

Serves 6

1.5 kg/3 lb shoulder of lamb
2 cloves of garlic, peeled
    and crushed
finely grated zest of 1 lemon
2 tablespoons olive oil
2 teaspoons ground
    coriander
1 teaspoon paprika
salt and freshly ground
    black pepper

Preheat the oven to 150°C/300°F/gas mark 2.

Remove the lamb from the fridge and wipe it with a paper towel. Combine all the other ingredients to make a paste and rub it over the lamb. Cover and refrigerate for at least 3 hours but preferably overnight.

Put the lamb in a roasting pan, add 1 cup of water and cover with aluminium foil. Place in the oven and cook for 3 hours. Reduce the temperature to 120°C/250°F/gas mark 1 and cook for a further 3 hours. When cooked, let the meat stand for at least 10 minutes. Shred the meat with a fork.

Serve on a bed of mashed potato.

poultry

Poultry in Ireland

Hens and the collecting of warm eggs from the nest were part of my early experience when visiting my grandmother's house. Even on a day trip, to be asked to go to the hen house and collect some eggs was a treat. The hens on Granny's farm, like many other Irish farms of my childhood, had an idyllic existence of roaming the yard freely and retreating to the cosy hen house as necessary. They ate luxuriously on scraps from the table and the fat worms from the soil. This rich diet resulted in egg yolks almost orange in colour. Soft-boiled eggs and soldiers of buttered toast for dipping into the middle were utterly delicious, considering their simplicity. Eggs, for me, represent a glorious association with my childhood and just the thought of a simple boiled egg can transport me to times past.

Keeping hens was traditionally the woman's task and selling the eggs provided added income. Hens were kept for their egg-laying capacity and were central to Ireland's rural economy during the nineteenth century. Bartering was common between a country woman and the local grocer, and eggs would be exchanged for tea, sugar and flour.

Hens have also traditionally been food for the table. Easy to rear and easy to slaughter, farmyard poultry was a ready food source and part of the Irish food culture since medieval times. For those living in more urban settings, roast chicken was a meal to be enjoyed on special occasions, due in some part to the cost of it, which made poultry almost a luxury item in the towns.

Ducks, geese and turkeys are also specially reared for the pot and are increasingly popular on weekly domestic menus, especially duck. Turkey and goose are still the festive choice at Christmas, with extraordinary numbers being prepared for that market.

Poultry has become a convenience food in recent years with versatile cuts that appeal to the diet-conscious, such as skinless breasts of chicken. There has also been a rise in sales of pre-cooked chickens. This is mainly due to the installation of large rotisserie ovens in most food stores, making the lives of working parents everywhere easier. Getting a hot nutritious meal on to the table after a hard day's work is easy with a cooked chicken. All this demand has created a highly competitive chicken industry that has given rise to the great chef and producer debates on what's best for the chicken. While they slug it out, point for point, the consumer has been left dazed and confused.

My heartfelt policy is: Irish bred, Irish reared and Irish prepared. It is my consistent view and I assure you it is based purely on quality and taste rather than patriotism. Integrity and best practice are hallmarks of the strict Irish code of chicken breeding and it is one of the best in the world. I have personally visited many of the chicken producers in Ireland and have found excellence at all times; even when dropping in unannounced as I often like to do. Yes, indeed, some chickens see more of the great outdoors, particularly on the small organic farms, but those rearing chickens on a larger scale are also passionate about what they do.

When it comes to Irish-produced chicken, the only difference I can see between organically raised or free-range chickens and those reared predominantly indoors is the husbandry; and I fully appreciate that it may be the most important choice criteria for some.

On the other hand, on a large-scale farm, the chicks to be raised are bought from the same hatchery as those to be reared organically or as free-range. They are fed on a carefully measured diet of wheat, barley, soya bean, meal and maize, and are constantly monitored throughout the day. The temperature of their houses is kept at optimum throughout the life of the chicken, with water and feed available on demand. While we tend to think that the chicken would love to pop outside at will, the reality is that chickens like to be warm and, as we all know, the average Irish temperature for most of the year is not exactly tropical.

When they are ready for slaughter, they are collected in the very early morning and are ready for the shops in a matter of hours. The meat could not be fresher and the hygiene and work practice are of the highest standard.

There is a choice available to the Irish shopper of corn-fed, free-range or organic, and each is a matter of taste. Corn-fed poultry are raised conventionally with a high corn content being present in their diet. They are clearly different in colour, taking on a golden tinge resulting from the feed.

'Free-range' means that the chicks are given access to an outside run, allowing them to roam and forage. They are fed a natural diet similar to all other chickens. Because of the costs and time involved with the free-range regime, the end product on the shelves is considerably more expensive than conventionally reared poultry.

As a matter of interest, I have undertaken numerous taste tests with those whom I regard as having discriminating palates. Rarely can the meat be identified as clearly one or the other. A number of small producers are bringing a uniqueness to the market with specific breeds and a longer growing period, which is great. I am very happy to stand over the quality of all Irish chicken. We have marvellous controls in place and I'm very confident that our indigenous producers will continue to comply with the rigorous standards demanded. Just remember: Irish bred, Irish reared and Irish prepared – it is ultimately about nutrition at the end of the day. After that, it is a matter for your personal beliefs and your pocket; your taste buds will benefit whatever you choose.

Handling Chicken

Chicken is consumed in extraordinary quantities in Ireland. Easy and quick to cook for the time-strapped, chicken is also regarded as an excellent choice for the diet-conscious, especially the skinless cuts that are readily available. However, raw chicken is susceptible to bacteria and particular attention to storage and preparation is required.

Chicken must be stored in a fridge at all times. When defrosting a frozen chicken, allow it to do so overnight in the fridge. Chicken must be completely thawed to be safe to cook and, once thawed, should be cooked within twenty-four hours.

Use a separate chopping board when cutting chicken and wash immediately after use, along with any knives that are used. As with all food handling, hands should be washed before and after handling chicken.

Chicken must be cooked thoroughly. Check for doneness with a thermometer, or by piercing the thickest part of the meat with a skewer. Juices released should have no trace of pinkness, but run clear.

Chicken as Medicine

Anyone who has ever had a cold, let alone a nasty winter flu, will no doubt have been told to eat chicken soup. Some believe the chicken soup theory to be just an old wives' tale and that any warm, thick liquid is comforting when ill. They have a point, but chicken soup is also known as Jewish penicillin and has been proven scientifically to have therapeutic properties when it comes to colds and flus. However, such a statement should be amended to say that 'home-made' chicken soup can help with a cold or flu, since it is the fat in the chicken that holds the flu-fighting compounds. Sadly, the additives and salt in many of the dried packet soups negate any medicinal properties.

Poultry Recipes

Chicken is perhaps one of the most versatile foods on the planet and the whole world seems to know it. Chicken is as popular in the east as it is in the west, be it found in a

curry in India, covered with plum sauce in China, deep fried in breadcrumbs in America or casseroled in Europe. It is sold in as many ways as there are ways to cook it. It is very popular with those watching their weight, since it is lean.

While portions are certainly convenient, buying a whole chicken offers much better value. With a whole bird you can take it home and conjure with it in several different ways until you get to the end of it: roasted, cold with salad, sandwiched, souped and finally turned into stock for the freezer. OK, the last suggestion is possibly aspirational, since few of us have the time to make our own stock these days, but do try it sometime as there is nothing quite as delicious as home-made stock for future dishes. I find it best to store stock in ice-cube trays in the freezer. The weather, however, often dictates the dish and there is something superbly warming about a hearty chicken casserole with loads of large, roughly chopped, rustic vegetables and creamy mash when frost covers the ground.

Chicken with Ham and Cheese Stuffing

Chicken breasts can sometimes be quite bland if left undressed. This is a quick and very easy way of cooking a chicken breast with a little surprise inside.

Serves 4

4 boneless, skinless
    chicken breasts
4 slices ham
4 slices Gruyère cheese
salt and pepper
3 tablespoons plain flour
1 tablespoon olive oil
15 g/½ oz butter
½ cup sherry or white wine

Flatten the chicken breasts by placing them between clingfilm or greaseproof paper and pounding with a rolling pin. Lay out the chicken pieces and place a slice of ham and cheese on each. Season and then fold over the chicken piece to make a parcel. Pinch the edges and dust with the flour.

Heat the oil and butter in a heavy-based frying pan and place the chicken pieces carefully into the pan. Cook for 3 minutes on each side and then add the sherry or wine. Continue to cook until the chicken is done, which will take 10–15 minutes depending on size.

Remove the chicken to a platter and reduce the sauce if necessary. Pour the sauce over the chicken to serve.

Chinese Chicken Noodle Soup

This soup is delicious, nutritious and low in calories.

Serves 6

1 medium chicken

fresh ginger, peeled and cut into 12 matchsticks

salt and pepper

2 tablespoons sesame oil

1 tablespoon olive oil

6 cloves of garlic, peeled and cut into slivers

3 cups chicken stock

1 packet dried egg noodles (thin)

1 cup broccoli, cut into small pieces

handful of spinach leaves, shredded

1 cup oyster mushrooms, sliced thinly

4 spring onions, finely chopped

Place the chicken in a large saucepan, add the ginger and cover with water. Poach gently for 1 hour or until cooked. Remove the chicken from the pot, reserving the liquid for stock. Remove the skin from the chicken and shred the chicken meat. Place it into a bowl, adding the seasoning and sesame oil. Allow to stand for an hour or so for the flavours to develop. Meanwhile heat the olive oil and fry the garlic slivers until well browned and crunchy. Set the garlic aside.

In a large saucepan add the 3 cups of stock and cook the noodles until soft. Add the broccoli, spinach and mushrooms. Cook for 6 minutes, then add the shredded chicken and stir.

Dish up into bowls and garnish with the garlic and spring onions.

Coq au Vin (Rooster in Wine)

This is a classic French dish. While that sounds fancy, it is simply a delicious chicken casserole with a red wine sauce.

Serves 6

1 medium chicken

2 medium carrots, peeled and sliced

2 celery stalks, sliced

18 shallots, peeled and left whole

1 bouquet garni made with a bay leaf, 4 sprigs of thyme and 4 sprigs of parsley tied together

1 tablespoon coarsely ground black pepper

1 bottle red wine

4 tablespoons olive oil

2 tablespoons plain flour

200 g/7 oz streaky bacon rashers, chopped

350 g/12 oz small mushrooms

fresh herbs, chopped, to garnish (optional)

Preheat the oven to 180°C/350°F/gas mark 4.

Place the chicken, carrots, celery, shallots, bouquet garni and pepper into a large bowl. Pour over the wine. Leave it to stand overnight or at least for a few hours in the fridge.

Drain the chicken and vegetables, reserving the wine. Pat dry the chicken pieces. Heat half the oil in a heavy-based frying pan. Add the chicken and brown well all over. Remove the chicken to a casserole dish. Add the carrots, celery and shallots to the pan and cook for 5 minutes or so until lightly coloured. At this point stir in the flour and gradually add the reserved wine and bring to the boil, stirring constantly. Pour this mixture directly over the chicken. Cover and cook in the oven for 1 hour or so until the chicken is tender.

Meanwhile, heat the remaining oil in a pan and fry the bacon pieces for a minute or so, before adding the mushrooms for a further 5 minutes. When the chicken is cooked, remove the casserole from the oven, add the bacon and mushrooms and sprinkle with freshly chopped herbs if desired.

Braised Herb Chicken

I always try to use tarragon for this as it combines really well with chicken, but any fresh herb will work.

Serves 6

30 g/1 oz butter
2 cloves of garlic, peeled
    and finely chopped
2 tablespoons fresh tarragon,
    chopped
salt and pepper
1 medium chicken
1 tablespoon olive oil
1 cup chicken stock
150 ml/5 fl oz cream

Preheat the oven to 200°C/400°F/gas mark 6.

Mix together the butter, garlic, tarragon and seasoning. Separate the skin of the chicken from the meat at the breast and fill the space with the butter mix, spreading it over the meat.

Heat the oil in a large cast iron casserole and brown the chicken all over. Add the chicken stock and cover tightly. Cook in the oven for 1½ hours or so until the chicken is cooked.

Remove the chicken from the casserole, cover it and leave it to rest. Strain the sauce and return it to the casserole. Simmer until the sauce reduces and thickens. Add the cream, adjust the seasoning and serve over the sliced chicken.

Chicken Korma

I love korma for its rich, creamy texture. While it is considered a type of curry, it is very mild.

Serves 6

1 medium onion, peeled
  and chopped
2 cloves of garlic, peeled
  and chopped
3 tablespoons sunflower oil
3 tablespoons plain flour
2 tablespoons korma curry
  powder
750 g/1 lb 10 oz boneless,
  skinless chicken breasts
1 tablespoon fresh coriander
  plus extra for garnish
2 tablespoons seedless
  raisins
350 ml/12 fl oz chicken
  stock, warmed
30 g/1 oz flaked almonds
juice of ½ lemon
2 tablespoons natural yoghurt
2 tablespoons double cream
salt and black pepper

Fry the onion and garlic gently in the oil in a large frying pan for about 5 minutes, or until soft. Mix the flour and curry powder in a large bowl. Cut the chicken into 2.5 cm/1 inch cubes and toss them in the powder mixture until evenly coated. Add the coated chicken to the pan and fry, stirring, for about 3 minutes. Add the coriander to the chicken with the raisins and stock. Bring to the boil, stirring. Reduce the heat and simmer for 10 minutes.

Toast the almonds in a dry frying pan. When the chicken is cooked, remove the pan from the heat and stir in the almonds, lemon juice, yoghurt and cream. Add salt and pepper to taste. Reheat very gently, but do not allow it to boil.

Garnish with the reserved coriander and serve with rice.

Chicken Fricassée

Fricassée is the Irish method of preparing a very tasty stew-like dish which is finished with an egg and cream sauce.

Serves 6

1 lemon

1 medium chicken

1 medium carrot, peeled and quartered

1 large onion, peeled and quartered

bouquet garni of a bay leaf, a sprig of thyme and a few parsley stalks

8 black peppercorns

1 cup milk

3 cups water

Sauce

50 g/2 oz butter

50 g/2 oz plain flour

570 ml/20 fl oz cooking liquor

1 egg yolk

60 ml/2 fl oz double cream

2 leeks, sliced thinly

salt and pepper

Garnish

6 streaky bacon rashers, chopped

2 tablespoons olive oil

110 g/4 oz mushrooms, thinly sliced

1 bunch watercress

Place the lemon inside the chicken cavity and secure the legs to keep them in place and then put the chicken into a large saucepan. Add the rest of the ingredients and simmer for an hour or so. Test for readiness by removing chicken from the pot. When pierced, the juices should run clear.

To make the sauce add the butter to a large saucepan and melt over a low heat. Add the flour, blending it into the melted butter. Remove from the heat and add the liquor (i.e. the cooking sauces), a little at a time, stirring constantly to keep it free from lumps. Return to the heat and stir until thickened. Meanwhile, boil the leeks for 5 minutes in salted water, then drain. Mix the egg yolk with the cream and add this mixture to the sauce. Season to taste and then add the drained leeks, mixing well. Do not allow the sauce to boil.

Fry the bacon in the oil until crisp and drain on kitchen paper. Add the mushrooms and cook for a few minutes.

Cut the chicken into serving portions and lay on a serving platter. Cover with the sauce and garnish. Serve with rice, baby potatoes or crusty bread.

Chicken Cotoletta

This dish is hugely popular in Italy, where the recipe has been handed down verbally from generation to generation. This is my version.

Serves 4

2 boneless, skinless
  chicken breasts
1 cup fresh breadcrumbs
1 teaspoon dried oregano
½ tablespoon Parmesan
  cheese, finely grated
2 cloves of garlic, peeled
  and crushed
½ cup parsley, finely chopped
salt and pepper
50 g/2 oz plain flour
2 eggs, beaten
½ cup olive oil

Cut the chicken into pieces and flatten into thin steaks. In a bowl, combine the breadcrumbs, oregano, cheese, garlic, parsley and seasoning. Place the flour on a plate and the beaten eggs in a dish and dip the chicken pieces into the flour, then the eggs and then the breadcrumb mixture. Refrigerate for an hour or so if possible.

Heat the oil in a frying pan and cook the chicken for a few minutes on each side until golden brown. Drain on kitchen paper and serve immediately with boiled potatoes.

Chicken with Forty Cloves of Garlic

Yes, forty cloves of garlic – that's not an error, but it's not as fiery as it sounds. When roasted the garlic becomes mellow and sweet. You'll be glad to see that the cloves don't have to be peeled!

Serves 6

2 sprigs of rosemary
2 sprigs of flat-leaf parsley
2 sprigs of thyme
1 lemon
40 cloves of garlic, unpeeled
1 large chicken
2 tablespoons olive oil
salt and black pepper
1 medium carrot, peeled
   and chopped
1 large onion, peeled and
   quartered
1 cup white wine

Preheat the oven to 200°C/400°F/gas mark 6.

Put the herbs, lemon and 10 or so garlic cloves into the chicken cavity. Brush the chicken with the olive oil and season with salt and pepper. Put the chicken into a large cast iron casserole dish. Add the carrot, onion, wine and remaining garlic. Cover securely and cook for 1½ hours or until the chicken is tender.

Lift the chicken from the casserole and strain the juices through a sieve. Remove the garlic cloves from the sieve and discard the rest of the vegetables. Boil the juices for a few minutes to reduce and thicken a little. Cut the chicken into portions and spoon over the juice and garlic cloves. Serve with crusty bread to soak it up.

Tipperary Chicken with Apples

County Tipperary was once known for its abundance of apple orchards. Canny Tipperary farmers always kept a few apple trees in order to supply the family with fruit and provide the necessary ingredients for a little apple liqueur.

Serves 6

3 cooking apples, peeled
   and cored
1 tablespoon lemon juice
2 tablespoons olive oil
1 medium chicken, jointed
   into 6 pieces or 6 chicken
   legs
1 medium onion, peeled
   and finely chopped
1 celery stalk, finely chopped
1 tablespoon plain flour
80 ml/3 fl oz Calvados
2 cups chicken stock
30 g/1 oz butter
125 ml/4 fl oz crème fraîche

Finely chop 1 apple into small dice, and the other 2 into wedges. Toss in the lemon juice.

Heat the oil in a pan and add the chicken pieces. Cook until golden brown, adding a little more oil if necessary, then remove from the pan and keep warm. Add the onion, celery and diced apple and cook for 5 minutes or until wilting but not browned. Remove the pan from the heat and sprinkle in the flour, stirring to combine. Add the Calvados and return to the heat. Gradually stir in the chicken stock. Add the chicken to the pan and simmer for 30 minutes or so, until the chicken is well cooked.

In another pan heat the butter and add the apple wedges. Cook until browned and tender.

Remove the chicken from the pan and add the crème fraîche to the liquid. Bring to the boil and cook for 5 minutes or so until the sauce is thickened. Season and spoon over the chicken. Garnish with apple wedges.

Chicken Cacciatore

In Italy, where this dish is considered a classic, it is called 'Hunter's stew'.
That name alone tells us all we need to know about this warm, satisfying dish.

Serves 6

2 tablespoons olive oil

6 chicken thighs

1 medium onion, peeled
and finely chopped

2 cloves of garlic, peeled
and crushed

½ cup dry white wine

1½ tablespoons white wine
vinegar

½ cup chicken stock or water

1 x 400 g/14 oz can tomatoes

2 tablespoons basil,
chopped

1 teaspoon sugar

salt and pepper

3 anchovy fillets

¼ cup milk

50 g/2 oz black olives

2 tablespoons parsley,
chopped

Preheat the oven to 180°C/350°F/gas mark 4.

Heat the oil in a heavy-based pan and brown the chicken all over. This should take about 10 minutes. Remove the chicken from the pan and place in an ovenproof dish. Pour off most of the pan juices and add the onion and garlic. Cook until the onion is soft and aromatic. Add wine and vinegar and boil until reduced by half. Add the stock or water and cook for 2 minutes or so.

Push the tomatoes through a sieve and add the liquid to the pan with the basil, sugar and seasoning. Cook for 5 minutes or so, until well combined and simmering, then pour the tomato mixture over the chicken. Cover and cook in the oven for 1½ hours.

Meanwhile soak the anchovy fillets in the milk for 5 minutes, drain them and chop into small pieces. When the chicken is cooked, remove it from the oven and arrange the pieces on a serving dish and keep warm. Pour the juices into a saucepan and bring to the boil for 1 minute.

Add the anchovies to the pan along with the olives and parsley, pour the sauce over the chicken pieces and serve with pasta.

Cream of Chicken Soup

Chicken soup made with a whole chicken and enjoyed as a meal is the perfect food for a busy lifestyle. Any vegetables can be added to this dinner in a bowl.

Serves 6

1 medium chicken
2 litres/3½ pints water
2 large onions, peeled and
	finely chopped
4 sticks celery, sliced
85 g/3 oz butter
1 parsnip, peeled and
	chopped
3 tablespoons plain flour
salt and pepper
chicken stock cube (optional)
½ cup cream
parsley, finely chopped,
	to garnish

Put the chicken into a large saucepan and add the water, one of the chopped onions and half the celery. Bring to the boil, reduce the heat and simmer, covered, for 1½ hours or until the chicken is cooked. Now remove the chicken from the stock and save the stock.

In a separate pan, melt the butter and add the remaining chopped onion and celery and the parsnip. Cook gently until the onion is tender. Add the flour and stir until combined. Cook for one minute or so. Return to the heat and continue to stir until the soup boils and thickens. More water may be needed, depending on the consistency of the liquid. Season with salt and pepper and a crumbled stock cube if using. Cover the pan and continue to simmer for 10 minutes or so.

Remove the meat from the chicken and add to the soup. Add the cream and heat through. Do not allow the soup to boil. Sprinkle parsley over each bowl of soup.

Chicken Satays with Peanut Sauce

I love this as it is low effort for a great taste reward. If you are making this for children, you might want to leave the chillies out of the sauce.

Serves 6

2 boneless, skinless chicken
    breasts (each breast will
    make 4 satays)
3 tablespoons soy sauce
2 tablespoons honey
2 cloves of garlic, peeled
    and finely chopped
1 tablespoon brown sugar
1 tablespoon sunflower oil
sliced cucumber for garnish
8 satay sticks (soaked in
    water to prevent burning)

Peanut sauce

6 tablespoons crunchy
    peanut butter
3 tablespoons sesame oil
2 tablespoons soy sauce
2 tablespoons honey
2 cloves of garlic, peeled
    and finely chopped or
    crushed
1 tablespoon lemon juice
    (to taste)
1 red chilli, deseeded and
    finely chopped (optional)

Cut each chicken breast into 4 strips. Combine the soy sauce, honey, garlic and sugar in a bowl and mix together, then add the chicken. Marinate for an hour or so.

Thread the chicken on to the satay sticks. Heat the pan (a chargrill pan is ideal, but a frying pan will do) and add the oil. Cook the satays for 3 minutes, turning to prevent them sticking to the pan. Serve with slices of cucumber and peanut sauce.

To make the peanut sauce, combine all the ingredients and mix well to incorporate. If the sauce is too stiff, thin it with milk or a little water. Place the sauce in a small dish.

Lina's Duck and Pasta

This is one of my favourite dishes, handed down to my wife Lina by her own mother. The fat from the duck seeps through the pasta, making it a delicious, moist plateful of comfort.

Serves 6

2 cloves of garlic, peeled
    and crushed
1 teaspoon salt
pinch of ground black
    pepper
pinch of ground bay leaves
1 teaspoon caraway seeds
1 duck
200 g/7 oz fresh tagliatelle
fistful of raisins and stoned
    prunes

Preheat the oven to 190°C/375°F/gas mark 5.

Mix the garlic with the salt, black pepper, ground bay leaves and half a teaspoon of caraway seeds. Wash the duck inside and out. Dry it with kitchen paper and rub it inside and outside with the spice mixture. If possible, leave it for an hour in the fridge.

Cook the pasta until soft but still firm – don't overcook it. Mix the pasta with prunes and raisins.

Clean the outside of the duck with kitchen paper to prevent the spice mixture burning during cooking. Stuff the duck with the pasta and secure the cavity with cocktail sticks. Sprinkle the duck with the remaining caraway seeds. Put the duck into a roasting tin and roast for 2 hours.

To serve, quarter the duck and serve it with the tagliatelle from the cavity.

Duck with Plum Sauce

This is an easy recipe that I often cook with the juicy plums I get from nearby Apple Farm, where luscious plums are part of the offer in summer.

Serves 4

4 duck breasts
1 large red onion, peeled
    and finely chopped
500 g/1 lb ripe plums,
    stoned and quartered
2 tablespoons redcurrant jelly
salt and freshly ground black
    pepper

Prick the duck skin all over with a fork to release the fat during cooking. This will also help to give a crisp result. Heat a heavy-based pan and place the duck skin side down. Cook the skin side for about 5 minutes, turn the breasts and cook the meat side for a further 5–7 minutes, or until the skin is golden brown and the breasts cooked right through. Remove the duck and keep it warm. Pour off all but 2 tablespoons of duck fat, add the onion and fry until aromatic. Add the plums and cook for a further 5 minutes, stirring constantly. Add the redcurrant jelly and mix well. Return the duck to the pan and cook until heated through. Season with salt and pepper.

This goes very well with rice but can be served on a bed of creamy mash instead.

Christmas Turkey with Cranberry Sauce

My favourite time of year has to be Christmas. All through my life the build-up to the special day was phenomenal and as a butcher's child it was definitely a time of 'all hands on deck'! That week before Christmas always seemed long and hard, but my mother would encourage us to focus on 6.00 p.m. Christmas Eve, when our family celebrations would begin.

The first hint of Christmas was the string of fairy lights that appeared, draped around my mother's little office. Turkeys, geese and mountains of cured hams and bacon stacked in the cool room created an atmosphere of feasting and abundance. The shop was always full and the chatter was excited. In addition to the regular customers we had a mail-order business that grew year by year. To this day the smell of candle wax transports me back to Christmas as a child, when my mother wrapped endless parcels of meat in brown paper, tied them with string and sealed the knot with melted wax to secure it completely. A cluster of stamps completed the package and it was then posted, usually to the UK. Cured bacon was sent to relatives abroad who couldn't get home for Christmas. Reflecting on the difficulties attached to the service, I totally appreciate the speedy twenty-four-hour Internet delivery service we provide today and the insulated chilled box that we use to dispatch orders. No candle wax or string in sight!

Midnight Mass meant that we could lie in on Christmas morning. It was the one day in the year when the cattle would be fed later than the usual 9.00 a.m. Our year was one of constant routines, as it has to be when you farm animals, and the different schedule of Christmas Day was a luxury in itself. The wafting aroma of the turkey as it cooked for hours and hours guaranteed that we were well ready for the feast when it was finally dished up.

The cooking of the turkey was always the big issue for my mother on Christmas Day and the decision of how best to cook it, according to the latest wisdom, was part of the ritual of the meal. The big fear always was dry meat and all sorts of strategies were adopted to overcome such a fate. One year the turkey was cooked upside down, the next year on its side and another year consistently basted every half hour or so. There was much drama attached to the tenderness and moistness at carving. It almost seemed to prevent my mother and many other Irish cooks, I'm sure, from being able to enjoy the day until the meal was over. And yet in my memory I only remember great meals, so the fear of dry meat was unfounded.

This anxious obsession that so many Christmas cooks have with cooking the perfect turkey led me to find a timer that we now distribute free to our customers. It pops when the turkey is ready and has taken the stress out of cooking turkey, allowing everyone to serve meat that is cooked to perfection.

My mother always made a fresh chestnut stuffing for the turkey, although today you can substitute vacuum-packed prepared chestnuts or puréed tinned chestnuts if necessary. Dripping was used in the past, but oil and butter are normally used today.

Serves 10

1 turkey, size of choice
   (allow 225 g/8 oz per
   portion raw weight)
150 g/5 oz butter
½ cup olive oil

Stuffing
(makes 10 portions)
½ cup olive oil
1 medium onion, peeled
   and finely chopped
500 g/1 lb chestnuts or
   equivalent if using vac pac
chicken stock to cook
   chestnuts (optional)
1.5 kg/3 lb sausage meat
turkey liver, finely chopped
   (optional)
150 g/5 oz fresh breadcrumbs

Preheat the oven to 200°C/400°F/gas mark 6.

Weigh the turkey when it is stuffed and ready to cook. Allow approximately 15 minutes per 500 g/1 lb. Make the stuffing by heating the oil in a pan and frying the onion until aromatic but not brown. If using fresh chestnuts, make slits on both sides using a small knife and boil the chestnuts in water for 10 minutes. Drain and remove the outer shell and skins while the chestnuts are still warm. Cook the chestnuts in a little water or stock for about 5 minutes and then drain. Chop into small dice and combine in a bowl with the cooked onion and the rest of the ingredients. Stuff the turkey and place any leftover stuffing into a loaf tin.

Lift the skin of the turkey by pushing your fingers between the meat and the skin from the neck over the breast, and insert the butter to lubricate the turkey throughout the long cooking process. Place the turkey on a baking tray on its side, and coat with the oil. Cover the tin with

Christmas Turkey with Cranberry Sauce cont'd.

3 tablespoons parsley,
    finely chopped
salt and pepper

Cranberry sauce
400 g/14 oz cranberries
½ cup water
¼ cup orange juice
50 g/2 oz sugar

aluminium foil and roast for 30 minutes, then turn the turkey on to its other side, basting well with the pan juices. Baste the turkey every 30 minutes throughout the cooking process. Thirty minutes before cooking is completed, turn the turkey breast side up, baste well and return to the oven without the foil to allow the skin to become crisp. Cover the turkey with foil and rest it for at least 15 minutes before carving.

To make the cranberry sauce, simmer all the ingredients in a covered pan until the cranberries are soft. The cranberry sauce can be made in advance and kept in a sterile jar. It also makes a lovely Christmas gift.

Traditional Roast Goose

In Ireland in times past goose was central to any feast and was often the choice at Christmas, wedding feasts and the old tradition of Michaelmas celebrated on 29 September and St Martin's Eve on 11 November, neither of which seem to be of any significance today. Because Michaelmas coincided with the apple harvest, apple cider was a natural and fitting accompaniment.

As with all other animals, no part of the goose was wasted and goose soup, goose gravy and goose drisheen would be on the menu for days after the feast. Today goose fat is the popular foody fat of choice for cooking roast potatoes.

When choosing a goose for the table, it needs to be considered that the size of the goose can be deceptive, and allowance needs to be made for the low meat yield.

Serves 6

5 kg/11 lb goose
500 ml/18 fl oz chicken stock
salt and pepper
knob of butter

Stuffing
2 tablespoons olive oil
500 g/1 lb onions, peeled
    and finely chopped
3–4 fresh sage leaves,
    chopped
2 cups fresh breadcrumbs
200 g/7 oz sausage meat
2 egg yolks
salt and pepper

Preheat the oven to 220°C/425°F/gas mark 7.

To make the stuffing, heat the oil in a large pan and add the onions, cooking until translucent. Add the sage leaves and stir for a minute or so, and then tip the mixture into a bowl. Add the breadcrumbs, sausage meat, egg yolks and seasoning.

Prick the skin of the goose and insert the stuffing into the cavity. Tie the legs tightly and place the goose in a roasting pan and roast for 40 minutes. Reduce the temperature to 180°C/350°F/gas mark 4 and cook for a further 2 hours, or until the juices are clear. Baste the goose every 30 minutes throughout the cooking process.

Remove the goose and rest on a warmed platter, covered with aluminium foil, for at least 15 minutes. Pour off any fat from the pan (keeping it for roasting potatoes) and deglaze with the chicken stock, scraping any bits from the pan and incorporating them into the sauce. Adjust the seasoning and whisk in a knob of butter to enrich the sauce for a great result. The gravy could be strained for a perfectly clear result, or left a bit lumpy, which is how I like it.

game

Hunting and shooting game are long-established pastimes in Ireland, and the result is a wide variety of feathered and furred animals for the table. Gone are the days when a local commerce was established, with hunters selling their bag through the local butcher. Today only EU-accredited suppliers are allowed to provide game meat to the retail trade. It is possible, of course, to find locally shot game, but it can only be as a gesture or gift and not for financial gain.

Many large estates in Ireland rear ducks, pheasants and partridges which are hatched in confinement and released at six to seven weeks. After twelve weeks in the wild they are 'fair game' for the shoot. The season for ducks is 1 September to the end of January and at this stage supply is adequate to feed the demand, although it is on the increase.

Pigeon is also gaining in popularity, although mainly for the restaurant trade. Because pigeons cause significant crop damage to peas, beans, cabbages and corn, they can be shot out of season (1 November to the end of January) when deemed a pest.

Rabbit is a game meat that is seeing a huge increase in demand. Wild rabbit is available in Ireland, with cooks keen to use both the cuts of haunch and shoulder or whole rabbits for roasting. Unlike most other game, rabbits do not benefit from being hung, as the flavour is unique and fully developed. In fact, rabbit meat should be chilled as soon as possible. The best rabbit is medium sized and nearly grown. Old buck rabbits can be tough and would need long, slow cooking.

Pheasant must be hung in order to develop the taste. In times past, when rules and regulations were non-existent, it was not uncommon to see a brace of pheasant hanging behind a door or from the rafters. Now controlled, chilled conditions are required, with hanging for four or five days before plucking regarded as optimum.

Snipe and woodcock can also be found in certain specialty retail outlets in Ireland. The woodcock is a migratory bird from Scandinavia that finds Ireland warm and desirable in the winter, providing sport for hunters in the process.

Venison

The sounds of rifle shots in the mountain forests of Tipperary are not uncommon; the hunting season means that wild deer are plentiful. There has always been an abundance of deer in Ireland, which have been eaten with enthusiasm, as evidenced by the number of pits used for cooking deer that can be found at many archaeological digs across the country. These pits were in use from at least 2000 BC and were the method for cooking venison until the seventeenth century. From that time the consumption of venison was associated with the 'big house', where antlers were proudly displayed as proof of marksmanship.

Venison is a dark, close-textured meat with very little fat and what fat there is should be firm and white. A prime cut such as haunch, loin or fillet is best served rare. Because the meat is very lean it needs to be larded or wrapped in fat. The haunch is best roasted, and the shoulder benefits from long, slow cooking, as in braising or stewing.

Roast Venison with Red Wine Sauce

Because all venison in Ireland is from the wild, there is an intensity of flavour and firmness of meat that make it a very tasty option. Overcooking venison should be avoided, as it is a meat almost devoid of fat and a marinade that includes oil is essential when cooking the leaner cuts. Juniper berries are a natural partner for venison.

Serves 6

1 leg of venison
2 tablespoons melted butter
6 bacon rashers
1 heaped teaspoon cornflour
½ cup beef stock

Marinade
300 ml/10 fl oz red wine
150 ml/5 fl oz olive oil
bouquet garni made from a
    strip of orange peel, a
    bay leaf and a sprig each
    of parsley, thyme and
    rosemary, tied together
3 tablespoons red wine
    vinegar
1 medium onion, peeled
    and finely chopped
1 cinnamon stick
10 juniper berries
10 black peppercorns

Preheat the oven to 180°C/350°F/gas mark 4.

Combine all the marinade ingredients and mix well in a bowl large enough to hold the meat. Leave the meat to marinate overnight. When ready to cook, remove the joint, dry it well, and brush with the melted butter. Lay the rashers over the leg and place the joint in a roasting tin. Cover the joint with aluminium foil and roast for about 30 minutes per 500 g/1 lb plus 15 minutes more.

Strain the marinade and simmer over a low heat until it has reduced by half. Thicken with the cornflour, which has been mixed with the beef stock, and add to the sauce along with juices from the cooked venison.

Rest the meat for at least 15 minutes before carving, and serve with potatoes and red cabbage.

Venison Casserole
with Cranberries

Just like any meat swimming in rich juices, this tends to be a warming, hearty meal most suited to cold winter days.

Serves 6

3 tablespoons olive oil

1 large onion, peeled and
    finely chopped

2 celery sticks, sliced

2 teaspoons allspice

1 tablespoon plain flour

750 g/1 lb 10 oz venison,
    cut into 2.5 cm/1 inch
    cubes

225 g/8 oz cranberries

grated zest and juice of an
    orange

3½ cups beef stock

2 medium carrots, peeled
    and sliced

salt and pepper

Heat the oil in a cast iron casserole dish. Add the onion and celery and cook for about 5 minutes or until softened. Mix the allspice with the flour and place in a plastic bag. Put the cubed meat into the bag and shake well to cover the meat.

Remove the cooked onion and celery from the casserole, and add a little more oil if required. Add the venison pieces and cook until browned and sealed. Add the cranberries, orange zest and juice to the casserole with the beef stock and stir well. Add the carrots, the cooked onion and celery and heat until simmering. Cover with a tight-fitting lid and simmer for an hour or so or until the venison is tender, stirring occasionally. Season well before serving.

Perfect with mashed potatoes or champ.

Game Pie

Any full-flavoured gamey meat is perfect for this pie. Rabbit, venison or pheasant work equally well, or how about trying a combination?

Serves 6

2 tablespoons vegetable oil

2 leeks, sliced

2 parsnips, peeled and sliced

2 medium carrots, peeled and sliced

1 fennel bulb, sliced (optional)

750 g/1 lb 10 oz game meat

2 tablespoons plain flour

½ cup red wine

1 cup chicken stock

salt and pepper

3 tablespoons parsley, freshly chopped

1 packet puff pastry, thawed

1 egg yolk, beaten

Preheat the oven to 220°C/425°F/gas mark 7.

Heat the oil in a large pan and add the vegetables. Cook for about 10 minutes, stirring frequently. Remove the vegetables from the pan and add a little more oil if required. Add the meat to the pan in batches, browning well before removing. Sprinkle the flour into the pan and stir in a little of the red wine to make a paste. Add the remaining wine and the stock, stirring constantly to avoid lumps. Return the meat and vegetables to the sauce, add seasonings and parsley and simmer for 20 minutes or so until well cooked.

Spoon the mixture into a pie dish. Roll out the pastry and cover the mixture well, making sure that the 'lid' of pastry is bigger than the dish. Press down the edges and trim off overhanging pastry. Press the pastry well around the rim of the dish and brush with the egg. Make a small hole in the centre of the pie to allow steam to escape. Bake for 25 minutes or until pastry is risen and golden.

Boozy Rabbit with Prunes

I have been generously given this recipe by a friend of mine who is a rabbit aficionado and a very good cook to boot.

Serves 4

3 tablespoons olive oil

8 rabbit portions
   (2 for each person)

1 medium onion, peeled
   and finely chopped

3 cloves of garlic, peeled
   and finely chopped

4 tablespoons brandy

1½ cups red wine

1 tablespoon light brown
   sugar

250 g/9 oz ready to eat
   prunes

200 ml/7 fl oz cream

salt and pepper

Heat the oil in a heavy-based pan and fry the rabbit portions until golden brown on all sides. Remove the pieces and keep them warm. Add the onion and garlic and cook until softened. Return the rabbit to the pan, add the brandy and ignite it. When the flames have died down, pour in the wine. Stir in the sugar and prunes and cover, simmering for 30 minutes or so until meat is tender.

Remove the rabbit and keep the pieces warm. Add the cream to the sauce and simmer for 5 minutes. Season to taste. Return the rabbit to the pan, stir and serve.

Roasted Pheasant with Garlic

Pheasant is a very lean meat, so it's necessary to help it a little in the fat department to maintain moisture during cooking. Several strips of bacon across the breast during roasting help the meat to remain moist and succulent.

Serves 4

1 pheasant
salt and pepper
4 stalks of parsley
30 g/1 oz butter
6 streaky bacon rashers
6 shallots, peeled
6 cloves of garlic, unpeeled
    and left whole
1 teaspoon plain flour
125 ml/4 fl oz chicken stock
    (cube added to water if
    necessary)

Preheat the oven to 200°C/400°F/gas mark 6.

Rub the pheasant with salt and pepper and fill the cavity with the parsley and butter. Tie the legs together and tuck the wingtips under. Place in a small roasting tin and lay the bacon over the pheasant to prevent it drying out. Scatter with the shallots and garlic and roast for 25 minutes. Remove the bacon and roast for a further 10 minutes.

Remove the shallots and garlic. Remove the legs from the pheasant. Put the legs back into the tin and cook for a further 5–10 minutes, then remove from the oven.

To make the gravy, transfer the baking tin to the hob over a low heat. Stir in the flour and cook for a few minutes. Add the stock and bring to the boil, whisking constantly. Boil for 2 minutes to thicken slightly, then strain the gravy. Serve the pheasant on a platter with the shallots and garlic scattered over the top, with gravy on the side.

Pan-fried Pheasant Breast with Mustard

The delicious crust and berry jelly add interesting layers of taste and texture to the pheasant meat, while the sauce makes for a lovely moist dish.

Serves 4

4 skinless and boneless pheasant breasts
3 tablespoons redcurrant jelly, melted
1 cup fresh breadcrumbs
30 g/1 oz butter
1 tablespoon olive oil
2 tablespoons wholegrain mustard
300 ml/10 fl oz cream
salt and pepper

Brush the breasts with the melted jelly and then press the breadcrumbs into the pheasant. If time allows, refrigerate for an hour or so.

Heat the butter and oil in a pan and cook the pheasants over a high heat to ensure the crumb coating is golden brown. Reduce heat and cook for 5 minutes or so.

Combine the mustard, cream and seasonings in a bowl, pour over the pheasant and simmer for 10 minutes until cooked through.

Champ

Potato Gratin

Potato Wedges

Potato and Onion Casserole

Puréed Parsnips

Carrot and Parsnip Mash

Carrots with Crème Fraîche

Garlic Spinach

Leeks with Bacon and Cream Sauce

Cauliflower with Cheese Sauce

Barbecued Asparagus with Garlic Mayonnaise

Baked Tomatoes with Garlic Butter

French Beans with Almonds

Broad Beans with Bacon

Grilled Courgettes with Pine Nuts

Corn Fritters

Roasted Vegetables with Couscous

Braised Red Cabbage with Apples and Wine

side dishes

My primary focus is meat and delivery of premium meat to my customers. However, as part of the effort to provide a complete service, we have a very busy section of the shop that offers salads, cold meats, pies and ready-to-go meals for people in a hurry. The range of salads includes the constant favourites – coleslaw and potato salad – plus an ever-changing choice that ranges from broccoli and carrot, beetroot and sour cream, roasted vegetables and couscous.

Until recently side dishes might just be a few vegetables; always potatoes, cabbage and usually carrots and turnips. There was only one way to cook them and that was 'boil until soft', except for the Sunday roast when root veggies would be bunged into the oven.

Today the range of vegetables offered has been extended from tomatoes, corn, cauliflower, broccoli, asparagus and so on to exotics such as red pepper, aubergine and courgettes. A well-chosen side dish truly enhances the star of the meal, the meat, also improves the appearance and visual appeal of the meal while providing another layer of taste.

Champ

This is an Irish standard to accompany almost any dish, but is especially good when served with a 'wet' dish, for soaking up the gravy. I like to use British Queens in summer, Kerr's Pinks in autumn and, in winter, Golden Wonders.

Serves 6

1 kg/2 lb 4 oz floury
   potatoes
300 ml/10 fl oz milk
85 g/3oz butter
6 spring onions, finely
   chopped
salt and pepper

Simmer or steam the potatoes until soft, then drain off the water and let them stand for a few minutes. Heat the milk in a small saucepan and add the butter. Add the spring onions and turn the heat off to allow the onions to infuse. Mash the potatoes and add the milk mixture. Season to taste, adding more butter if you fancy it.

Potato Gratin

This certainly makes something special out of plain old potatoes.

Serves 6

6 large potatoes, peeled
1 litre/35 fl oz milk
salt and pepper
35 g/1¼ oz butter
300 ml/10 fl oz cream
1 cup Cooleeney Farmhouse
   Cheddar cheese, grated

Preheat the oven to 180°C/350°F/gas mark 4.

Place the potatoes in a saucepan with the milk and seasoning. Bring to the boil and simmer for a few minutes until the potatoes are just beginning to soften when pierced with a fork. Drain the potatoes and slice into thin slices. Melt the butter and pour over the base of a baking dish. Layer the potatoes in the dish and pour the cream over them. Top with the grated cheese and bake for an hour or so or until the top is golden and crusty.

Potato Wedges

These are an ideal, satisfying accompaniment to a perfectly grilled steak.

Serves 6

6 large potatoes, peeled
2 tablespoons olive oil
1 teaspoon paprika
salt and pepper

Preheat the oven to 180°C/350°F/gas mark 4.

Cut the potatoes into wedges. Run the potatoes under cold water, drain, and dry well with a paper towel. Place the potatoes into a clean plastic bag and add the oil and paprika. Shake and massage the potatoes with the oil/paprika mixture, then spread on to a baking sheet. Sprinkle with salt and pepper and bake for 45 minutes or so, until the wedges are cooked through and crunchy.

Potato and Onion Casserole

Serves 6

6 large potatoes, peeled and sliced thickly
2 medium onions, peeled and sliced very thinly
salt and pepper
50 g/2 oz butter
1 cup beef stock

Preheat the oven to 180°C/350°F/gas mark 4.

Mix the potato and onion slices together and spread in a shallow baking dish. Sprinkle with salt and pepper. Cut the butter into small pieces and dot over the top of the vegetables. Add the stock and bake for an hour or so until the stock has been absorbed and the potatoes are cooked.

Puréed Parsnips

Parsnips aren't everyone's cup of tea, but this is a winning way to prepare them.

Serves 6

1 kg/2 lb 4 oz parsnips, peeled and chopped
salt
110 g/4 oz butter
pepper

Boil the parsnips in salted water until soft. Purée with the butter and additional salt and lots of pepper – delicious!

Carrot and Parship Mash

Make sure you properly mash the mash. No lumps allowed!

Serves 6

3 medium carrots, peeled and cut into rings
3 parsnips, peeled and cut into rings
110 g/4 oz butter
salt and pepper

Boil the vegetables in salted water until soft. Drain and mash well (or purée in a food processor for a really good result), adding butter and seasoning. More butter can be added according to taste, and I must say I do use considerably more than indicated here!

Carrots with Crème Fraîche

Serves 6

1 kg/2 lb 4 oz small carrots,
    peeled, topped and tailed
50 g/2 oz butter
salt
3 tablespoons crème fraîche
pepper
small bunch of chives,
    finely chopped

Put the whole carrots into a large saucepan, add the butter and cook over a low heat to glaze the carrots for a few minutes. Cover the carrots with water, add salt and cook for 15 minutes or so until the carrots are tender. Drain, then season, stir in the crème fraîche and serve with a sprinkle of chives.

Garlic Spinach

Spinach must be well washed and drained before cooking. Sandy grit is usually present even if the spinach is sold washed and ready to eat. It is always a surprise how much spinach reduces after cooking, so always cook more than you think you need.

Serves 4

2 bunches of spinach, well
    washed and drained
50 g/2 oz butter
3 cloves of garlic, peeled
    and finely chopped
salt and pepper

Place the spinach in a large pot of salted water and cook rapidly for 2 minutes. Drain well in a colander, pushing a fork into the spinach to remove as much moisture as possible.

In a pan melt the butter and add the garlic, moving it constantly to avoid burning. When the garlic is just beginning to turn colour, add the drained spinach and mix.

Leeks with Bacon and Cream Sauce

Leeks are possibly the dirtiest of vegetables, as they push through the earth bringing lots of grit between the leaves. The root should be cut off along with the tough green leaves.

Serves 6

3 bacon rashers, chopped
1 tablespoon olive oil
15 g/½ oz butter
6 leeks, cut into thin rings
salt and pepper
1 teaspoon paprika
1 cup sour cream
1 tablespoon lemon juice
2 tablespoons parsley,
    finely chopped

Fry the bacon in the oil until crisp. Set aside. Melt the butter in the same pan, add the leeks and cook until softened but not brown. Add the salt and pepper and the paprika and stir. Add the sour cream and lemon juice, and continue to cook until heated through. Add the bacon and parsley and serve.

Cauliflower with Cheese Sauce

If cauliflower cheese appeared as part of the Sunday roast, it always meant that my mother was in a cooking mood. It is almost a meal in itself, although as part of the roast dinner feast it adds something very special. Leftovers are delicious on toast.

Serves 6

1 large cauliflower,
    cut into florets

Cheese sauce
30 g/1 oz butter
1 tablespoon plain flour
1½ cups milk
salt and pepper
¼ teaspoon English mustard
    (dry or prepared)
pinch of nutmeg
½ cup Tipperary Jarlsberg
    cheese, grated

Preheat the oven to 180°C/350°F/gas mark 4.

Cook the cauliflower in boiling salted water until just tender. Drain and layer into a baking dish.

For the cheese sauce, melt the butter and remove from the heat to add the flour. Cook for a few minutes, stirring constantly. Add the milk, continuing to stir until it reaches boiling point. A whisk makes easy work of this, ensuring no lumps.

Season with salt and pepper, add the mustard and nutmeg and simmer for 5 minutes or so. Remove from the heat, add the cheese and stir until well mixed.

Pour over the cauliflower and bake for 30 minutes.

Barbecued Asparagus with Garlic Mayonnaise

Usually lightly boiled in salted water for a few minutes, asparagus can be trans-formed by the addition of a drizzle of olive oil and a squeeze of lemon juice to finish it. Asparagus is also wonderful when grilled on the barbecue. A trim is usually required by cutting off the tough stalk.

Serves 6

2 bunches of asparagus
3 tablespoons olive oil
salt and pepper
4 cloves of garlic, peeled
    and crushed
4 tablespoons good-quality
    mayonnaise

Toss the asparagus in the oil and set it on to a hot barbecue or stove-top grill. Cook for 10 minutes, turning to avoid burning. Remove, place on a platter and sprinkle with salt and pepper. Stir the garlic into the mayonnaise and serve on the side.

Baked Tomatoes with Garlic Butter

Slow-roasting tomatoes is very simple and the bigger the tomatoes the easier they are to manage. They look colourful and very impressive when brought from the oven to the table on a baking tray.

Serves 6

6 beef tomatoes
4 cloves of garlic,
    peeled and crushed
110 g/4 oz butter, softened
½ cup fresh herbs, finely
    chopped
freshly ground black pepper
good-quality salt
3 tablespoons olive oil

Preheat the oven to around 150°C/300°F/gas mark 2.

Cut a small cavity in each tomato where the stalk has grown. In a bowl mix together the garlic, butter, herbs and pepper and place a teaspoon of the mix into each cavity. Place the tomatoes on to a baking tray and sprinkle with salt and the olive oil.

Roast for 1½ hours. Spoon the juices over the tomatoes before serving.

French Beans with Almonds

French beans can be a great addition to any meat dish when cooked simply. The trouble is that they are often cooked to death, losing colour, taste and, most importantly, texture. The beans should be cooked for just a few minutes in boiling water until tender, not soft, then drained immediately and run under cold water to stop the cooking process.

Serves 6

500 g/1 lb French beans
1 tablespoon olive oil
bunch of spring onions,
    finely sliced
1 clove of garlic, peeled
    and crushed
2 tablespoons slivered
    almonds
salt and pepper
squeeze of lemon juice

Prepare the beans by topping and tailing them. Leave whole and cook in salted water until just tender. Drain. Melt the olive oil in a large pan, add the spring onions and garlic and cook until tender. Add the almonds and cook until the almonds are golden brown. Add the beans, season, add lemon juice and cook until the beans are hot.

Broad Beans with Bacon

Broad beans are not readily available, but the frozen option is an excellent alternative.

Serves 6

500 g/1 lb broad beans
30 g/1 oz butter
1 small onion, peeled and
    finely chopped
3 bacon rashers, chopped
    into small pieces
2 tablespoons cream
salt and pepper
parsley, finely chopped,
    to garnish

Cook the beans in salted water until tender. Drain and set aside. Melt the butter in a pan, add the onion and cook for a few minutes, then add the bacon and cook until the bacon and onions are golden. Add the beans and the cream and season. Serve sprinkled with parsley.

Grilled Courgettes with Pine Nuts

Courgettes have very little flavour in their natural state but cooked on a griddle the flavours miraculously materialise.

Serves 6

4 courgettes, cut in lengths
    into thin slices
4 tablespoons olive oil
salt and freshly ground
    pepper
40 g/1½ oz pine nuts, lightly
    roasted

Brush each side of the courgette slices with olive oil and cook for just a minute or so on each side until the courgettes have black stripes. Platter up and drizzle with a little olive oil and seasoning, and finish with the pine nuts.

Corn Fritters

My children love these fritters, and they can be a meal in themselves, dipped in sauce. They are great as part of a barbecue or brunch.

Serves 6

15 g/½ oz cornflour

110 g/4 oz self-raising flour

1 egg, beaten

2 tablespoons milk

1 tin sweetcorn
    (approx 200 g/7 oz)

2 large spring onions,
    finely chopped

1 red chilli, deseeded and
    finely chopped (optional)

good-quality salt and freshly
    ground pepper

2 tablespoons olive oil

handful mixed herbs, finely
    chopped, or extra spring
    onions, finely chopped, to
    garnish

Mix the cornflour, self-raising flour, egg and milk until the mixture is smooth, then add the sweetcorn, spring onions, chilli (if using), salt and pepper.

Heat the oil in a frying pan and carefully drop in a large spoonful of corn mixture. Fry each side for about 3 minutes until golden brown. Sprinkle with salt and pepper. Can be served with satay sauce.

Pile on to a platter and top with finely chopped herbs or spring onions to garnish.

Roasted Vegetables with Couscous

This is easy to put together and is a brilliant side dish with any meat, but is particularly good as an accompaniment for barbecues. Roasted pumpkin makes this dish special and is a great way to introduce it into the vegetable range.

Serves 6

4 tablespoons olive oil

1 sweet potato, peeled and cut into cubes or thickly sliced

1 large potato, peeled and cut into cubes or thickly sliced

1 butternut pumpkin (squash), peeled and cut into cubes or thickly sliced

2 parsnips, peeled and cut into cubes or thickly sliced

2 medium carrots, peeled and cut into cubes or thickly sliced

1 large onion, peeled and chopped into quarters

1 whole garlic bulb left whole, sliced across the top of the cloves

salt and pepper

500 g/1 lb couscous

Preheat the oven to 180°C/350°F/gas mark 4.

Pour a little oil into the base of a baking dish and add the vegetables. Pour a little more oil over the top and mix. Roast for an hour or until the vegetables are well cooked through and slightly browned.

Prepare the couscous according to the instructions on the packet. Squeeze the garlic cloves out of the skins. Mix this purée through the vegetables then mix the couscous and vegetables together, adding seasoning to taste. Serve hot, or cold as a salad.

Braised Red Cabbage with Apples and Wine

In recent years this has been an addition to our Christmas feast.

Serves 6

50 g/2 oz butter
1 large onion, peeled and
   sliced thinly
1 red cabbage, cut into
   quarters, core removed,
   sliced as thinly as
   possible
3 Bramley apples, peeled
   and chopped into
   1.25 cm/½ inch dice
1 cup white wine
1 tablespoon sugar
salt and pepper

Melt half the butter in a pan, add the onion and cook until soft. Add the remaining butter, the cabbage and the apples and stir well. Add the wine, sugar and seasoning to taste, then cover and simmer for about 45 minutes. Serve hot. You can always prepare red cabbage in advance, as it is a dish that reheats quite well.

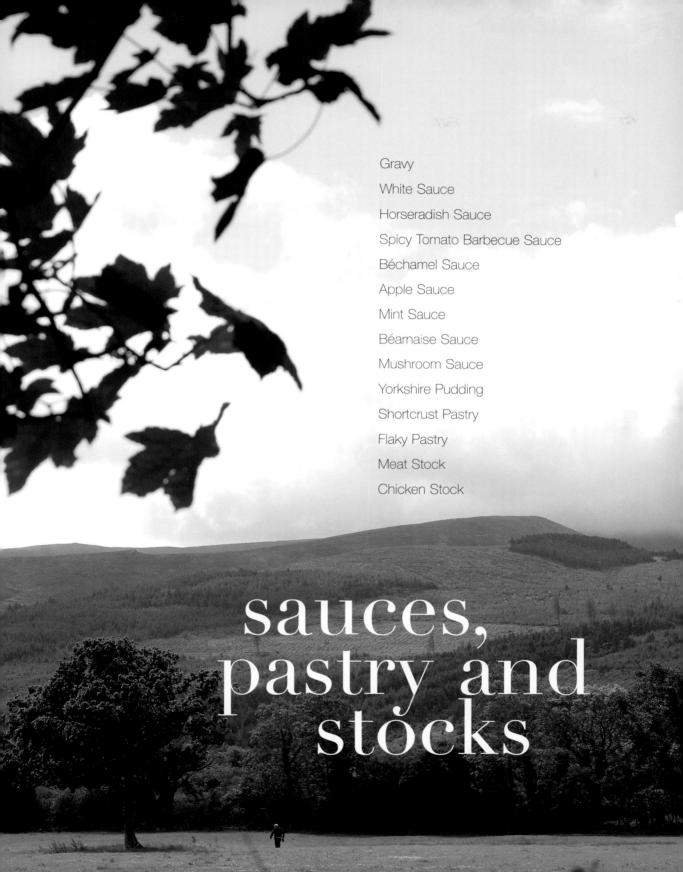

sauces, pastry and stocks

Gravy

1 stock cube dissolved
    in 1 cup of water or
    1 cup beef stock

Pour off all the fat from the roasting pan and reserve the pan juices and any sediment and scratchings from the meat. Add the stock. Place the roasting pan over a high heat and bring the stock to the boil, stirring continuously to dissolve and incorporate the meaty sediment. Add seasoning to taste. Strain and serve gravy as required.

White Sauce

30 g/1 oz butter
2 tablespoons plain flour
250 ml/9 fl oz milk
salt and pepper

Melt the butter in a saucepan over low heat and stir in the flour. Cook gently for 1–2 minutes and remove from the heat. Pour in the milk all at once, stirring continuously. Return to a moderate heat and bring to the boil, stirring, until the sauce thickens and bubbles. Season. A balloon whisk is the right tool for this job, and saves lumps developing.

Variations: Add 50 g/2 oz grated Cheddar and a pinch of cayenne pepper for a cheese sauce, or finely chopped parsley to make parsley sauce.

Spicy Tomato Barbecue Sauce

1 cup tomato ketchup

2 tablespoons white wine
   vinegar

1½ tablespoons
Worcestershire sauce

1 tablespoon grated onion

2 tablespoons olive oil

1 teaspoon sugar

salt and pepper to taste

1 clove of garlic, peeled
   and crushed

1 teaspoon paprika

½ teaspoon dry mustard

Mix all the ingredients together in a saucepan and bring to the boil over a low heat. Simmer gently for 10 minutes. This sauce is excellent as a basting sauce for barbecuing meat, or served as a sauce with sausages, rissoles and steaks.

Horseradish Sauce

250 ml/9 fl oz béchamel
   sauce

2 teaspoons cream

2 teaspoons sugar

1 tablespoon bottled
   horseradish relish or sauce

salt and white pepper

Make a béchamel sauce (see page 240). Add the cream, sugar and horseradish relish or sauce and stir well. Season to taste. Serve cold with roast beef.

Béchamel Sauce

1 cup milk

1 bay leaf

2 parsley stalks

6 peppercorns

1 shallot, peeled and finely
    chopped

1 small carrot, peeled and
    sliced

1 celery stalk, sliced

1 clove of garlic, peeled

30 g/1 oz butter

2 tablespoons plain flour

salt and pepper

2–3 tablespoons cream
    (optional)

Place the milk in a saucepan with the herbs, peppercorns and vegetables and bring slowly to the boil. Remove from the heat, cover and leave to infuse for 30 minutes or so.

Strain and discard the flavouring ingredients, saving the milk. Melt the butter in a small saucepan, stir in the flour and cook over a low heat for 1–2 minutes. Add the warm milk gradually and bring to the boil, stirring constantly to avoid lumps. When the sauce is thick and bubbling, add seasoning to taste. Add cream for extra richness if required.

Apple Sauce

3 cooking apples, peeled,
    cored and sliced

¼ cup water

1 teaspoon butter

sugar to taste

lemon juice to taste

Put the apple slices into a saucepan with the water. Cover and simmer gently until soft enough to mash. Stir the butter into the warm sauce and add sugar and lemon juice to taste.

Mint Sauce

2 tablespoons fresh mint,
  finely chopped
2 teaspoons sugar
1 tablespoon boiling water
2 tablespoons white wine
  vinegar

Place the chopped mint in a small bowl and add the sugar. With the back of a spoon, work the sugar into the mint to release the flavours. Add the boiling water and stir until the sugar dissolves, then add the vinegar. Stand for at least 30 minutes before using.

Béarnaise Sauce

125 ml/4 fl oz dry white wine
3 egg yolks
¼ cup tarragon vinegar
1 tablespoon parsley, finely
  chopped
1 tablespoon shallots,
  peeled and finely chopped
½ teaspoon dried tarragon
200 g/7 oz butter
½ teaspoon salt
freshly ground black pepper

Beat 1 tablespoon of the wine into the egg yolks and set aside. Combine the rest of the wine with the vinegar, parsley, shallots and dried tarragon in a saucepan. Cook over a low heat until the mixture reduces by one-third in volume.

Bring water in the bottom of a double boiler to a simmer and pour the reduced vinegar mixture into the top of the double boiler. Stir the egg yolk mixture into the wine, beating briskly with a whisk. Add the butter a little at a time, stirring until each addition melts and blends into the sauce. When the sauce is thick, remove from the heat, season with salt and pepper and strain into a sauceboat or similar.

Mushroom Sauce

30 g/1 oz butter
2 shallots, peeled and finely
    chopped
250 g/9 oz mushrooms,
    finely sliced
1 teaspoon lemon juice
2 tablespoons plain flour
¼ cup white wine
350 ml/12 fl oz cream
salt and pepper

Melt the butter in a frying pan, add the shallots and cook over a medium heat for a minute or so. Add the mushrooms and lemon juice and cook until the mushrooms are cooked and the liquid has evaporated. Add the flour and cook, stirring, for 2 minutes and then add the wine and 300 ml/10 fl oz of the cream and bring to the boil, stirring constantly until the sauce thickens. Remove the pan from the heat and stir in the remaining cream, adding seasoning to taste. Adjust the thickness of the sauce by adding more wine if necessary.

Yorkshire Pudding

110 g/4 oz plain flour
pinch of salt
1 egg
250 ml/9 fl oz milk

Oven temperature 240°C/475°F/gas mark 9.

Sift the flour and salt together into a mixing bowl.
Make a well in the middle and add the whole egg.
Add half of the milk, a little at a time, and gradually stir
in the flour from the sides of the bowl, using a wooden
spoon. Beat the batter for 5–10 minutes until air
bubbles appear. Cover and stand for 30 minutes,
then stir in the remainder of the milk.

When the meat is cooked, remove the joint from the
oven and rest it in a warm place. Use a little of the oil
from the roasting tin to grease muffin tins. Turn the oven
to 240°C/475°F/gas mark 9 and pour the batter into
the tins so that the mixture comes halfway up the sides.
Cook the Yorkshire puddings in the oven until they are
golden and crisp, around 20 minutes or so. Serve
immediately with roast beef.

Shortcrust Pastry

175 g/6 oz plain flour
125 g/4½ oz cold butter,
    cut into cubes
1 egg yolk
approximately 3 teaspoons
    iced water

Sift the flour into a bowl and rub in the butter until the mixture resembles breadcrumbs. Alternatively, process in a food processor. Add the egg yolk and just enough water to bind the dough together, then press it into a ball and knead lightly on a floured surface. Wrap in clingfilm and refrigerate for at least 30 minutes.

Flaky Pastry

350 g/12 oz plain flour
pinch of salt
225 g/8 oz cold butter
1 teaspoon lemon juice
cold water to mix

Sift the flour and salt into a bowl. Divide the butter into 4 parts and rub one portion into the flour with your fingertips. Add lemon juice and enough cold water to make a soft dough. Roll out the dough to a rectangle. Mark the pastry dough into thirds lightly with a knife. Cut one portion of the butter into little bits, and sprinkle over two-thirds of the pastry. Sprinkle a little flour over the dough and fold a third over the middle third, and then the other third on top of that. Press the edges together and roll out again into a rectangle, and repeat with the butter portion cut into little bits and sprinkled on to the dough, which is then folded in on the centre. Repeat again, cover with clingfilm and refrigerate for at least 30 minutes. Use as required.

This is the key to a superb steak and kidney pie, apart from the excellent quality of meat, of course!

Meat Stock

The most delicious meat soups, stews, casseroles, gravies and sauces rely on a good home-made stock for success. Neither a stock cube nor a canned consommé will do if you want the best flavour. Once made, meat stock can be kept in the refrigerator for 4–5 days, or frozen for longer storage.

Serves 6

2 kg/4½ lb beef bones, such as shin, leg, neck and clod or veal
2 medium onions, unpeeled and quartered
2 medium carrots, peeled and roughly chopped
2 celery stalks, roughly chopped
2 tomatoes, roughly chopped
4.5 litres/8 pints cold water
handful of parsley stalks
few sprigs of fresh thyme
2 bay leaves
10 black peppercorns, slightly crushed

Preheat the oven to 230°C/450°F/gas mark 8.

Put the bones in a roasting tin or flameproof casserole and roast, turning occasionally, for 30 minutes or until they start to brown. Add the onions, carrots, celery and tomatoes and baste with the fat from the tin. Roast for a further 20–30 minutes or until the bones are well browned. Stir and baste occasionally.

Transfer the bones and vegetables to a stockpot. Spoon off the fat from the roasting tin. Add a little of the water to the roasting tin and bring to the boil on top of the stove, stirring well to scrape up any browned bits. Pour this liquid into the stockpot and add the remaining water. Bring just to the boil, skimming frequently to remove all the foam from the surface. Add the parsley, thyme, bay leaves and peppercorns. Partly cover the pot and simmer the stock for 4–6 hours. The bones and vegetables should always be covered with liquid, so top up with a little boiling water from time to time if necessary.

Strain the stock through a sieve. Skim as much fat as possible from the surface. If possible, cool the stock and then refrigerate it: the fat will rise to the top and set in a layer that can be removed easily.

Chicken Stock

1 whole chicken
1 onion, peeled and quartered
2 celery stalks, chopped
2 leeks, chopped
6 black peppercorns
1 stalk parsley

Wash the chicken under cold running water and place it in a heavy-based large pot. Cover with water, bring to the boil and reduce to a simmer. Add remaining ingredients and cook for about 2 hours.

Strain the stock and allow it to cool. Remove any fat that has set on the surface at this point. (Chicken fat in stock has properties that are believed to assist the healing process.)

Index

crumbed lamb cutlets, 147
curries
  chicken korma, 170
  Kashmiri lamb curry, 125

dip: Persian lamb meatballs with aubergine and
    yoghurt dip, 141
duck
  duck with plum sauce, 184
  Lina's duck with pasta, 183
dumplings: beef stew with dumplings, 65

eggs: bacon and egg pie, 94

filo pastry: pork filo pie, 110
flaky pastry, 246
  steak and kidney pie, 41
French beans with almonds, 228
fricassée: chicken fricassée, 173
fritters, corn, 231

game
  game pie, 199
  recipes, 197–207
  see also pheasant; rabbit; venison
garlic
  baked tomatoes with garlic butter, 227
  barbecued asparagus with garlic mayonnaise,
      223
  chicken with forty cloves of garlic, 175
  garlic spinach, 219
  poached leg of lamb on white bean and
      garlic purée, 146–7
  roasted pheasant with garlic, 205
goose: traditional roast goose, 190–1
gravy, 238
  red wine, 42–3
Guinness: braised beef and Guinness casserole,
    46

ham
  chicken with ham and cheese stuffing, 165

cider-glazed ham, 113
  pea and ham soup, 97
haricot beans: pork and beans, 104
herbs
  braised herb chicken, 169
  braised lamb shanks with rosemary and
      balsamic vinegar, 144
  lamb steaks with rosemary, 127
  roast lamb with herb stuffing, 140
  roast leg of lamb with lemon and rosemary,
      128
  rolled herb pork with crackling, 105
horseradish sauce, 239

Irish stew, 134

jus, red wine, 122–3

Kashmiri lamb curry, 125
kebabs
  beef satay, 61
  chicken satays with peanut sauce, 182
  lamb kebabs, 137
kidney beans, red: chilli con carne, 64
kidneys: steak and kidney pie, 41

lamb
  apricot-stuffed lamb, 132
  barbecued leg of lamb, 152
  braised lamb shanks with rosemary and
      balsamic vinegar, 144
  crumbed lamb cutlets, 147
  Irish stew, 134
  Kashmiri lamb curry, 125
  lamb and potato pie, 148–9
  lamb kebabs, 137
  lamb shank soup, 133
  lamb steaks with rosemary, 127
  moussaka, 131
  navarin of lamb, 124
  Persian lamb meatballs with aubergine and
      yoghurt dip, 141

Notes

AN IRISH BUTCHER SHOP